BACK OF BEYOND

BACK
OF BEYOND

BY

S.L. BENSUSAN

WITH AN INTRODUCTION BY

ROGER A. FREEMAN

Illustrated by Joan Rickarby

BLANDFORD PRESS
LONDON NEW YORK SYDNEY

First published in the UK 1945 by Blandford Press Ltd.
This Javelin Books edition first published 1988
Artillery House, Artillery Row, London SW1P 1RT

Distributed in the United States by
Sterling Publishing Co., Inc.,
2 Park Avenue, New York, NY 10016

Distributed in Australia by
Capricorn Link (Australia) Pty Ltd,
PO Box 665, Lane Cove, NSW 2066

British Library Cataloguing in Publication Data

Bensusan, S. L.
   Back of beyond : a countryman's pre-war
   commonplace book.
   1. North Essex. Rural regions. Social
   life, ca 1920-1939. Biographies
   I. Title
   942.6'7083

I S B N 0–7137–2060–3

Printed in Great Britain by The Guernsey Press Co., Guernsey C.I.

INTRODUCTION

BY ROGER ANTHONY FREEMAN

Ancillary to his farming business, my father ran a large retail milk round during the 30s and early 40s. In the school holidays I was frequently directed to accompany the girls who drove the milk vans; not my favourite task and always performed under protest. The delivery round to which I was mostly assigned traversed the village of Langham, very much a 'long village', which extended from the borough boundary of Colchester north to the bank of the river Stour, separating Essex from Suffolk. On one occasion as the girl stopped the Austin Seven van opposite a small group of council houses, a man was walking towards us on the other side of the lane.

'That's Mr Bensusan – the author!' she exclaimed in a hushed voice, 'You know, the one that writes all those clever books.'

I cannot now honestly bring to my mind's eye a likeness of this man, whether he was large or small, young, old, or anything of his physical appearance. The encounter is remembered only for the reverence in the girl's voice, signifying this was no ordinary gentleman. I doubt if she had read any of his works but, nearly fifty years ago, a published author resident in a rural area tended to be looked upon as a celebrity. Moreover, although a 'furriner' and thus the subject of suspicion, he was at the same time revered for his benevolence and because he chose to write about country matters.

Sam Bensusan came to Nightingale Lane, Langham, in the early 30s, renovating a cottage and removing the residue of a poultry farm spread across a small valley between two woods. He had lived in other homes in rural Essex, but one guesses that the Nightingale Lane property was near the long sought-after ideal, possibly a retreat for eventual retirement. A prolific writer on a wide range of subjects – he had ultimately some sixty books and a prodigious number of newspaper and magazine articles to his credit – with rural matters nearly always his dominant and best-loved theme. For many years a regular contributor of agricultural and countryside notes to *The New Statesman*, he was probably better known for his delightful rural stories in the *Morning Post* and, later, the *Manchester Guardian*. Sam Bensusan's activities also extended to broadcasting, concentrating there too on the country scene. Nevertheless, his interests were as diverse as his writing experience was considerable. Sixty years around Fleet Street had brought him associations with some of the literary giants of his time; notably Wells, Hardy and Kipling.

Back of Beyond is mostly the story of the establishment of home and garden at Nightingale Lane and the measure of life lived in this, then quiet, corner of Essex. The narrative follows the seasons and the changing face of nature through observations of flora and fauna recorded in near poetic phrase. Here was a gentle heart, enthralled by the beauty of his valley, understanding the cruelty of nature but never quite coming to terms with its violence.

The narrative of *Back of Beyond* reveals much of the author's own philosophy and, in particular, his disdain of urban encroachment and its spoilation of the countryside. Much of what he writes is still applicable; at times it is easy to forget that he writes of days a half century and more gone by.

The peace of his back-of-beyond sanctuary was not to last. With the Second World War – the time when this book was compiled – a searchlight unit was installed in the ragwort and rabbit infested meadows next to the stream. Later, an airfield was torn out of farmland to the south and the flight path from the main runway lay right over the house. The enemy also contributed to the disturbance; a flying bomb detonated in the woodland. Sadly, post-war, advancing years and ill health forced a move to a less demanding residence on the south coast where he died, aged 86, in December 1958.

There are still a few Langham inhabitants who recall Sam Bensusan, a big, moustached, round-faced man, crowned with a trilby, who would pass the time of day with anyone. They still talk of what, to many, were his eccentricities, such as his disbelief in and refusal to attend funeral services. Nor have they forgotten his generosity to the village and, in the pre-war days of rural poverty, his discreet benevolence to wanting individuals. However, Sam Bensusan's finest bequest was the wealth in his writings, which stand as testimony to a caring man: prose holding the wonders witnessed around green acres of bygone England. Few writers have achieved it so beautifully.

ROGER ANTHONY FREEMAN
FEBRUARY 1988

CONTENTS

CHAPTER I

BY WAY OF INTRODUCTION

1.—How It Came About.

WE had wintered in Rome and I sat with the Local Authority in a quiet corner of the Borghese Gardens on a February afternoon talking of an outlook that seemed to hold little promise for those whose life-road runs downhill. England had lately gone off gold, the lira was laughing rather contemptuously at our shrunken Treasury Notes ; our outlook was coloured by this contempt. "If a younger generation takes a great part of my work away, as it should and must,"

9

I told her, " we will do well to buy a small place in the country once more, a cottage with garden and orchard, a few acres, a place remote from highways." I quoted from a charming book . . . " I have an idea that there is somewhere, far away from here a certain little cottage . . . I think of a bench before a threshold and of fields spreading out of sight . . . I would like to have a fine garden and live on the edge of a wood."

The L.A. who, being countrywoman at the red ripe of the heart, has never suffered cities gladly, agreed at once. " We do know how to run a place," she mused aloud, as though memory of the first fifteen years of our married life had returned, with pictures of seed time and harvest, storm and sunshine, failure, success, and much happiness.

" There's no need to hurry home," I suggested, glad of her quick response. " We'll give the Spring time to reach England." So we surrendered again to the enchantment that is Rome, while on the hills of Veii, the sands of Ostia, and in the gardens that look down on Foro Romano we talked of a cottage that had not reached the plane of manifestation, a garden yet unmade, a district still undiscovered.

Several years have passed since then ; the home is not only in being but has asserted itself. Quite early I began to make note of simple happenings. They are the bases of this record of quiet, uneventful life before war fell on the world.

My scrap-book may perhaps hold an interest for those who, from the centre or even near the circumference of great cities, look for the day to dawn when they too may take the country road, and wonder what they will find.

In men who labour in towns under the stress of bitter competition there is ever a chord that must respond to the litany of green things growing, to bird song, to the story of any orchard when the bees make music amid its blossoms, of any hillside where the nightjar offers his little tribute of unearthly music to moon and stars. There must be moments, however brief, when the most sophisticated among us remembers the great Mother Earth from whom he came, to whom he must so surely and so speedily return, when he reminds himself how " swift from shine to shade the roaring generations flit and fade."

The world of anger and unrest seems shut out here. Meadow and stream and wood know nothing more than the urge of changing seasons, a part of their enduring peace enters into our lives.   So I have set down a rambling record for other simple folk who find pleasure in such recitals. There has been joy in the telling, and if my book adds even a few to the unknown friends who are every writer's reward, it will have been worth while.

2.—WHAT WE FOUND AND HOW.

You leave the main road, with its noisy litter of charabancs and motor-buses which are travelling south to London and north to Ipswich or St. Edmund's town, past countless uncouth efforts of the ribbon builder who has done so much to rob England of her pristine beauty.   By way of a forge, where an old-time blacksmith struggles bravely with ill-health and faces his diminishing tasks with a smile and a friendly word for all, you resume the country.   The road, secondary but cared for, declines to persist, content to merge in a pleasant lane.   Hedgerows draw close, there is no room for two farm carts to pass when you turn abruptly to the right.   Travel for nearly four hundred yards past a solitary rectory big enough to suggest that the church was once a power in the parish, follow on over what was a rough cart-track and is now a decent road to the edge of a larch plantation, and there, round the corner, past bungalow and garage, perched on a hill and looking from wood to wood, stands what has been in turn farmhouse, gamekeeper's home, farm labourer's cottage and poultry station.

When it was built, with ingle-nook fireplaces and broad supporting beams on a frame of oak or elm with wattle and daub beneath thatched roof, Charles I ruled or was about to rule over England ; Cromwell's Ironsides may well have ridden down the lanes to or from the siege of Colchester. In later years tiles replaced thatch, but since then no change had come to the cottage, which from the edge of its larch grove looked southward across a valley to yet a larger stretch of wood, oak and beech, chestnut and pine, ash and sycamore, now part of our small domain.   Here, far from crowds,

THE MEADOW

madding or otherwise, gamekeepers dwelt awhile in days when the rearing of pheasants was easier for landowners than it is or will be again. Before them were tillers of the soil; they have left old-fashioned clay drain pipes to tell of forgotten cornfields. In due season the last gamekeeper's place knew him no more. Poultry farmers came and went, dotting the shallow hill with unsightly chicken houses that cried aloud for some greenery to cover their nakedness if they might not be sold for what they would fetch to relieve a stricken landscape. And one afternoon, following four months of search for the country home that should offer the *trinoda necessitas* of woodland, stream and meadow, we came upon the cottage by lucky chance.

When first I sought such a place, I was very young, full of enthusiasm, well content with a home that lacked every modern claim to the title. Drinking water was brought twice weekly from a well half a mile away, in what my nearest neighbour, who acted as carrier and charged sixpence for his labour, called his " owd cowl." For light, oil lamps, for transport, bicycle or pony trap, for news—well, there was a man who sold papers in the little town only three miles away, and they were always there by the afternoon.   There was one post daily.   Rural telephone service was unknown ; gramophone unheard of ; ether preserved the secrets it has yielded since to the wireless set.   The soil was sticky clay that harnessed three horses to the plough and threatened to draw the boots off your feet ; men worked for ten shillings a week and were almost as cheerful as they were poor, because they had never known of a better life and the air was as stimulating as wine.   If even in those restricted circumstances the country appeared infinitely more attractive than the metropolis, what shall be said to-day, provided always that you can find the real unspoilt variety ?   It is becoming very rare within a seventy mile radius of London.

Three months after we had seen the cottage, builders and plumbers were giving it a new and unfamiliar lease of life. The Corporation six miles away had undertaken to deliver light and power, water was available from half a dozen springs. The Post Office had granted a telephone.   From Broadcasting House the bland announcer told what was happening in the great world, while I worked in field or garden or sat at my desk, a countryman who had recovered his freedom after nearly eight years hard labour—a monstrous sentence, unknown to English law and, like most human penalties, self-inflicted.

Through the first year of our married life we had been very happy in the country, the Local Authority and I.   We raised good crops, bred sound live-stock, planted orchards, made beautiful gardens and lived almost entirely on the fruits of the soil we cultivated.   Work at the Ministry of Agriculture took me from this home until the economy axe severed my connection with Whitehall and sent us back again, this time to the uplands of Essex.   But because prospects grew ill in farm land, because market-rings involved me in repeated loss and I was living to farm rather than farming to live, we decided to retire ; first, to a country town, and then to " Metropolis, whereunto the tribes of men assemble," with all the thrill and excitement of a return to the Street of

Adventure.　But there was always something amiss either with Metropolis or with us.　From late Spring and to early Autumn we made excuses to go away from London, and when Winter came, sought the Mediterranean.　At all seasons of the year, at all hours of the day the countryside was calling; the countryside that stands remote, that hides rare birds and shy animals, that ebbs and flows in flame of short-lived flowers. The land summoned us, the land over which the spirit of peace broods eternally, whether in the depth of winter days or when the night is no more than a swift wayfarer between sunset and sunrise.

When we surrendered to unseen voices and entered into our kingdom here, a tiny cottage with a handful of acres, we boasted no higher aim than to leave a space of Mother Earth more fruitful than we found it, to plant orchard and garden once more, to keep a little live stock, to make friends with all things that run and fly, save disturbers of the peace.　Apart from this interest in wild life we thought to prepare for the time when we may be called upon to grow what food we can, the time when our statesmen shall have rediscovered the country and learned that it holds cultivable land, men and women of great capacity, machinery and markets.

Save for a solitary farmhouse, we see only our own meadows and woods.　Visiting the cottage for the first time I heard my nearest neighbours; they dwelt invisible in the overgrown plantation nearby, a pheasant, a jay and two or three wood pigeons.　Later, in a fir tree top, I saw one far more attractive, the smallest of all our British birds, a gold crest.　He was alone and in the dull light the green and yellow and gold were not at their best, but the little fellow suggested the depths of the countryside, even to one who had seen him in Kew Gardens.

3.—ALTERATIONS.

I signed a contract with a builder living seventy miles away and engaged an architect who comes from twice that distance. Very soon my mind misgave me.　The specification provided for proper accommodation for the men, for a foreman, for all

THE JAY

manner of good things and effective arrangements, but most of these provisions were honoured in the breach.   Some workmen were engaged locally ; in moments of confidence they confessed that their association with the building trade was of the most casual kind ; looking back to-day I recall their confidences without enthusiasm ; they saw the joke that I paid for.   Sometimes the contractor felt compelled to leave them to their devices, sometimes the architect spent an hour or two on the place when the contractor, who had notice of his coming, would perhaps fetch him from the station, though intercourse between builder and architect lacked all affection, each being profoundly aware of the other's failure to reach perfection.   The three months suggested for the work became four, five, six, the conditions increasingly unsatisfactory. With shocking lack of appreciation for an immensely gifted young man who had put up with my innumerable shortcomings and had repressed the very justifiable contempt he must have felt for me, I told my architect that I felt the time had come to part company. He had already written to say that this job was the last he would carry out for me in any circumstances, a harsh but welcome decision, for it found us of one mind and had a prophetic quality that I recognised at once. An old friend on whom I can rely stepped into the breach and when the builders' accounts for extras advanced in force they suffered a frightful defeat—there were at least sixty per cent casualties. Let it be said to his credit that he faced the situation with a fine pluck and I called in a local man to set some of the crooked straight. More than a year and a half after his advent, he was still with us. Clients, he told me, had congratulated him on his speed, but I at least never joined the ranks of those who committed themselves in this fashion. Time the Devourer will soon tire of my generation, and I wanted to enjoy for a few years a cottage without a carpenter in attendance.

"Into the night go one and all "—builder, architect handyman, so far at least as I am concerned, but as Mr. William Shakespeare remarked : " The evil that men do lives after them " ; we were suffering from it several years later, but it did not amount to much. *Requiescant*.

4.—MAKING A HOME.

Now that home has taken definite shape, it is possible to say something more about the realisation of high hopes that came after we had driven delicately down the rough lane that keeps the cottage inviolate.

The place that needs no planning, no alterations, has several disadvantages. It is never quite yours. The man or woman who lavished thought, time and money upon it, retains certain rights not less definite because they lack foundation in law. Then again you must pay for improvements that were not of your choosing and even learn to love a ready-made garden. A man might accept almost any home ; given a quiet study and comfortable bedroom with bath nearby he would be content. But no woman could. Be assured that her predecessor had no sane ideas about cupboards, kitchen arrangements, passage room, lighting, heating, lavatory basins and the rest, while both man and woman, if they be garden lovers, will reject with contempt their predecessor's fads and fancies. So, in the long run, it is wise to start afresh.

As we found the cottage, it was homely to point of ugliness, lacking even a porch to hide the nakedness of a front door that opens into the narrowest passage to be found in the county. The design is of the kind one associates with a child's first architectural endeavour, carried out on a slate with a pencil, or on nursery floor with a box of bricks, but—fact of first importance—the foundations are on sand and gravel, not on the heavy clay dominant elsewhere. Rheumatism does not lie in wait, the cellar remains dry.

Simplicity was almost overpowering. A room to right and left of the front door, a flight of twisting stairs between, a room to right and left of the narrow landing, another short stairway leading to the attics. That was all, save for a cellar reached by stone steps.

Beyond the kitchen door was a shed with a few oak beams and what country folk call a bake-oven. Past the house the lovely view over valley to wood with its magnificent umbrage, was marred by an aggressive army hut over sixty feet long, next to it was a strongly built but needlessly ugly stable. Round the house on two sides the little fir wood holds north and east winds at bay, where the land falls southwards the mass of chicken houses, large, modern, well-fitted and more or less repellant, spoilt the view. There was not much in all this for the casual observer.

" You can't live in such a place," declared a friend with some approach to indignation. A near and dear relative begged the Local Authority to dissuade me from the purchase. " Do urge him to leave the place alone. You'll both come to hate it," she said with conviction. Both appeared richer in emphasis than imagination, but it was easy to understand the outlook. Fortunately, we already had our visions of the new cottage that would replace the old, we could realise the view that lay beyond the obtrusive army hut. We saw a study that could fill the site of the little brick-ovened shed, a garden that might arise in the fulness of even a short time from the tangle of what country folk call " culch "— docks, thistles, nettles, couch grass and coarse rank herbage then lying like a veil over the fair face of the hillside.   So we rejected the wise counsel of indignant or unhappy friends.

" He can't be living in a place like this," said a Great Lady to her chauffeur when she paid her first visit; " you must have gone wrong at the turning."   I retired out of earshot. " What a perfectly charming place," said the Great Lady when I came forward to greet her ; " you are so clever at finding these gems."

CHAPTER II

LOCAL TRADITION

5.—THE OLD FOLK.

IN all conversations recorded here the note of resistance to innovation and intrusion is stressed. I have endeavoured to set it on record because it will soon die down.

Only the old folk whose roots are in those Victorian days that few would describe as spacious, resent a progress that strikes at the roots of practice and prejudice, but they at least are conscious of the loss of something that the younger folk have never known. Tranquil hours through which men, the day's work done, laboured in their gardens and women at their needlework, their knitting and the rest of the handicrafts, are almost unknown to-day. A younger generation turns on the wireless and leaves it on, regardless of what is coming through, though a sense of selectivity compels some to cut out informative talks and news bulletins.

" I don't wanter to hear about furriners," declared a sturdy marshlander to me little more than a year ago. " I don't acquaint with sech ; gimme a band o' music all th' time."

No month passes without carrying away some of the old generation ; very soon the most of the folk who take their part in brief scraps of conservation will have been gathered to their fathers, sturdy men who started on a shilling a day— dying before an old age pension could bar the workhouse road.

I write largely of aged people and with full respect for their viewpoints, but I do not mourn good old times ; such things only exist in retrospect. If there were peaceful reactions, the day itself was long and difficult, yet under many burdens countrymen and women developed an individuality that tends to disappear. In a very few years, by the time the boys and girls are men and women not only the old forms of speech, but the old ways of thinking will have gone from the country I know best. Wages boards, wireless, cinema and daily papers will have shaped people into one pattern ; they may have some difference of political conviction, but it will not be founded on thought so much as on tradition.

" I allus vote yaller, bein' me father did," said my solitary Liberal neighbour long years ago. He did not know how an old age pension came his way ; it sufficed him to draw the money, and wonder whether those who paid him " come by it honest."

That great reservoir of rural individuality, the chapel, is losing its hold on the people because rigid Sabbath observance is a thing of the past. In the first village of my sojourn I offered to equip a cricket club for the lads who loafed through the Sunday afternoons and the parson told me in stiff, un-friendly tones, that he could not listen to such a suggestion and was shocked to hear it. He had already been compelled to protest against men working in their gardens on the Lord's day ; if this practice were not checked it would spread.

The fact that the farm worker had no more than the evenings when he came home worn out, did not affect the garden question nor did the absence of any half-holiday for boys engaged on the land. Rector, who was as straight as

he was narrow, took a long time to forgive me for my daring
suggestion. I doubt whether that forgiveness was complete
when he died and was succeeded by a man who kept bees and
cultivated an orchard, and consequently had broader views
and wider sympathies. He was one whose passing left marshland the poorer and robbed me of a good friend.

6.—The Modern Generation.

I have set out the reactions of elderly folk to modern
aspects of country life; the views of the younger generation
are harder to come by. It is possible to estimate the thoughts
behind the words of my own contemporaries, it is hard to
find in the outlook of the adolescents anything more certain
than an aversion from the country life. In many cases it is
the inevitable resentment against the cramping conditions
of the farm where the young man who is just twenty-one can
look to no better wages than he is taking now, if he serves
for the next forty-two.

It is easy to say that he is far better off than his father used
to be, that his grandfather did not earn in a month, without
half-holidays or regulated hours, as much as he can earn in a
week with a half-holiday thrown in. The hard fact is that
the young man never knew the harsh conditions of an older
time and, until the war, did not think the farm-worker's game
worth the candle.

" Not enough to do about here," says the village girl, and
goes off to the town, glad to work for long hours in stuffy
shops, restaurants, and offices for the sake of free evenings for
cinemas, dance halls, and a wide choice of young men.

It is silly to criticise their outlook, for criticism will neither
alter nor improve it. The most significant and heartening
fact in country life to-day is the quiet content of old folk who
know that, thanks to the Old Age Pension and perhaps the
Statutory Wage, they can stay in their chimney corner until
Father Time knocks at the cottage door with the summons
all must answer in turn. They have found happiness and
content ; will their successors be so fortunate ?

7.—The Parting of the Ways.

We are living at the parting of the ways ; one must travel far in this county of Essex, once so beautiful, to find a district that has not been urbanised. The younger generation has welcomed the change, it thinks in terms of " moty bikes," " grannyphones," and the wireless ; it hails charabanc and bus as deliverers from the tedium of a quiet life. The only plough that interests the boys is the one they can draw with a tractor, the only service to appeal to the girls is out of sight of the village.

It is left to the old folk, whose pension is to hand or in sight, to resent change and protest in their ineffective fashion against people from afar who invade territory once inviolate. I have had four homes in Essex, the first was found more than forty years ago, but in the eyes of the natives I have been, and must remain, an intruder, and there is no matter for resentment here. Village life was self-contained in the old days, men did not leave its narrow boundaries to find occupation, home, wife, or grave ; it was their world and filled their horizons. Where agricultural depression drove out one set of employers and brought another in place there was no advantage to be won, indeed there might he loss, for the newcomers would be far quicker to recognise the duty of the village to them, than their duty to the village. The old easy-going relations between employer and employed were modified, because employers did not understand the mentality of those who served them.

8.—" Furriners."

" People seem to suspect you here," said a friend who came to my marshland cottage. " Naturally," I told him.

The man who owns an estate is often a jealous landlord. The public has no access to his woods and gardens save on special occasions and for a specific purpose ; there are owners of quite insignificant property who do their best to obliterate rights of way, indifferent to the inconvenience this selfishness may create. They are responding to a universal possessive instinct, the feeling that makes the passenger look up with a sudden glance of annoyance when you invade his railway carriage, and makes six people in such a carriage do their best to look like ten. Now the countryman has his village and nothing else ; those who were there when he could first take notice are in a sense his brethren ; those who came a little later may be taken on sufferance ; late arrivals are intruders upon his privacy, aliens, suspects, " furriners." In this attitude the countryman and woman are but expressing a sentiment held just as strongly by others of a more fortunate social station. Throughout the world the Anglo-Saxon reaction to the newcomer used to be summed up in the old phrase, " Here's a stranger ; heave half a brick at him."

Mohammed gave special instruction to his followers, " to strangers and wayfarers be kind," but it has found small acceptance.

I remember once in Morocco giving civil greeting to a muleteer who passed me on the road. He responded with a curse, and I told my native servant to ask him why. The muleteer gave prompt and frank explanation. " If I were a rich man and powerful and I met strangers, I would cut many throats. But it has pleased Allah to make poverty my portion and I can do no more than say what is in my heart. Curse your religion." And with this, the most serious of all curses, the fierce sallow-faced, bearded Moor rode hastily on.

Between this man and the farm-worker who sees a stranger in the High Street he regards as his own, there is a close relationship. Each feels that his proper privacy is in danger.

In parts of Morocco before the French occupation no white man could venture, there were towns in the Atlas and even in more accessible parts that were called sacred. There are in other lands ceremonies that no stranger may witness. Our country men have no sacred cities, no secret ceremonies but they will keep very quiet indeed about certain customs and practices ; the stranger within their gates may have no part in them.

Some of this exclusiveness is associated with practices whose origin is lost. " We don't go where other folk belong," said one candid old countryman to me in the early pays of my sojourn in his village, when I protested mildly

against his suggestions that I had come down from " Lunnon "
to get away from the policeman on duty there. " An' we
don't want that other folk should come where we belong,"
he went on. " 'Tain't seemly."

9.—He Didn't Belong.

While many men who are farming here have come into
the country from elsewhere, the oldest families of Eastern
England are those of agricultural labourers, many of whose
names have been on the parish registers since first registers
were established.

" My gel married a furriner," said Mrs. Milt, the good
woman who worked for me more than thirty years ago.
" Me husban' was reg'lar upset; I thought that would lay
him on his bed o' sickness."

" Was your girl's choice a coloured man, then ? " I asked.

" Sakes alive," cried Mrs. Milt, " he worn't that kind o'
furriner."

" Where did he come from, then ? " I persisted, and she
named the village just two miles away. Had it been in the
next parish he would still have suffered the description.

In the village you belong or you do not belong ; there is
no middle way.

CHAPTER III

EARLY DAYS

10.—DISCOURAGEMENT.

I REMEMBER that before we had been here for more than a few weeks and on a stroll through by-ways that have at last become familiar, I encountered an elder, one for whom life held no illusions. Five feet high with small blue eyes, broad shoulders and a fringe of grey whisker he signalled me authoritatively to stop. Brief conversation ensued.

The Elder (slowly): "You're the gent what's bin an' bought th' owd cottage up the hill?"

The Scribe: "Yes."

The Elder: "Whatever fower?"

The Scribe: "I liked it."

The Elder: "Gooin' to live there, seem'ly?"

The Scribe: "Yes, that is the idea."

The Elder: "There ain't no garden."

The Scribe: "I noticed that. I'm going to make one."

The Elder: "You don't wanter trouble. Nawthen on't grow there, time you do."

The Scribe: "Who told you so?"

The Elder (emphatically): "I b'long to these parts."

The Scribe: "I'm going to grow first-rate flowers and fruit and vegetables. And I'm not going to use a ha'porth of minerals to do it with."

The Elder: "You're gooin' to waste y'r time an' y'r money. Telly f'r why. That land on't grow nawthen 'cept it's twitch an' culch (rubbish). Never hasn't. Everybody round here knows all about it."

The Scribe: "Wait and see."

The Elder (grimly): "I gotter wait, but I won't see. No more won't you. There ain't bin a garden there yet, an' there ain't goin' to be one this time o' day, t'ain't likely. If a man don't belong, he can't onderstand a place."

This last statement most unfeelingly reminded me of my lack of status, but it was natural enough. Here was a man who had lived in the village before any of the strangers had arrived. He felt that I was just another intruder.

I repeated the disconcerting interview to my gardener who is not of the county. "They've told me the same thing about here," he remarked contemptuously, "an' seeing how some of 'em work that don't surprise me. They couldn't grow anything here—or anywhere else." I felt sad to think that the elder could not hear that.

11.—MORE DISCOURAGEMENT.

There are quite a lot of these veterans, but I fear they can't help thinking that I am a bad thing to have about a place. Another one eyed me strangely as he stopped me in the lane a few weeks later.

"You're the gent what live on the hill top, ain't ye?" he began. I thought it best to admit my identity.

"I don't blaime ye f'r coming if so be you wanted to. But you on't grow nothin' up there, mind ye," he remarked, hitting an unoffending elder bush with his walking stick. "Howsomever, you kin buy what you want, an' you won't find any better air nowheres."

"Why won't things grow?" I asked.

"Because they never did," he replied succinctly. "Ain't I lived here man an' boy? Who should know if I don't, bein' I belong? But there," he added, by way of consolation as he hit the elder again, "folk don't die hereabouts."

"What do they do?" I enquired, walking to a point where he could no longer maltreat the bush.

"They wither, that's what they do," explained the old man, following me, to the elder bush's relief. "This air keeps 'em wonderful." He has "withered" since then and I miss him, for all that he held grave doubts about my *bona fides*. If he looked with suspicion upon folk who invaded his village, and in some cases sought to regulate the lives and thoughts of those they employ, can you blame him?

12.—HOW MUCH?

I found it a hard job to get a price named for services to be rendered. Perhaps the neighbourhood wished to take my measure before committing itself, or it may be that a bald

THE HARROW

statement of price smacks of indelicacy. Then, too, there is one figure for the native and another for the stranger within the gates, and while you know the first if you are a tradesman (the term is generic here), you have to guess the latter. I had to ask three people for a price for harrowing meadows before I could get a plain statement. Chain harrows were needed to break matted grasses, scarify mosses, clear rubbish and give grass a chance it had not enjoyed for years. I could see that sound meadows had been sacrificed to neglect. The first man applied to was discursive and defensive. Here is the conversation, condensed.

" Same as harrow y'r grass f'r ye ? "

" Yes."

" That ouldn't cost ye much. 'Tain't a long job."

" Twenty acres, as near as no matter. What would you charge ? "

" I'll charge ye a fair price, mind ye. You kin trust me right enough. Everybody round here'll tell you about me. I belong."

" I'm sure. What would your price be ? "

" Well, I shan't hurt ye . . . . "

I retired hurt none the less, and so did he, for he considered my failure to pursue the matter discourteous.

" He don't know what he do want, rightly speakin'," he complained to a neighbour.

My second application was hardly more fortunate. Here is the epitome.

" Have you a horse, a man and a chain harrow to spare ? "

" Yes, I think I have." I catch an underlying note of caution, of uncertainty. I had learned before applying that he was fully equipped with wordly wisdom, and that unless you knew precisely where you were going with him, he would land you in a ditch, not with malice but on principle.

" What will you ask to harrow my meadows ? "

" Well, I can't say. The best thing to do would be to let you have man and horse and charge by the day." Instinct told me he was thinking of winter keep ; I have noticed throughout the years of my pilgrimage that jobs carried out on the lines he proposed have the quality of the brook Tennyson wrote about. So I tendered grateful thanks, went still further afield and found a shrewd ex-farm bailiff who takes contract jobs and works at them.

" Can you harrow my meadows ? "

" Yes."

" When can you start ? "

" Any time, if you give me a week's notice."

" How much will you charge ? "

" . . . . Half-a-crown an acre for two horses, a man and a good chain harrow."

" Book the job." Since that far-off conversation the land has been properly harrowed and rolled, some of the old drains opened, the grass crop doubled.

13.—The Sparrows' Revenge.

When our first April came, cold and bleak, to the hill side, I decided that the sparrows should no longer be allowed to build under eaves in front of the cottage according to use and wont. They are the worst of neighbours. They get up with the sun to quarrel, fight and gibe at one another and at all birds that sing. They will not suffer house martins to approach. So their odds and ends of new building, ragged heaps of rubbish, were removed before even the first eggs were laid and the approach to their nesting ground barred by

weather boards. For three or four noisy mornings they held
indignation meetings on all parts of the roof, then retired
to the side of the wood, presumably to consider reprisals.
These took the form of daylight raids upon what we call
our lawn.

Long weeks of levelling had gone to its preparation, rolling
and seeding had followed and granted a little early rain, or
a fall of snow, of the kind that the country needed, all had
been well. But we suffered from many frosts and little rain,
harsh winds in place of snow, and sparrows with hearts full
of the spirit of revenge instead of more gracious sentiments.
The seed that germinated was well-nigh frozen, the residue
gave the sparrows some five regular meals a day and snacks
between, until what should have been a green expanse had
an unpleasant Sahara-like appearance with ragged oases here
and there. Only a flatterer could have called it a lawn, and
the sparrows deprived of their usual nesting place seem to
have multiplied as though exile were what they really needed.
Since then I have shouted at them, threatened them with guns,
poisoned grain, in short with every misfortune that can
befall a sparrow. But they chirp defiance and still return to
the side of the open window to watch the sun rise and remind
me that they at least are up.

14.—THE LAWN.

We have the worst croquet lawn in the county and are
proud of it. There is something a little depressing about
croquet, it dates you so definitely ; lawn tennis would sound
much more attractive. But when you have passed the time
for strenuous games and can only look on by the side of
court and cricket field, golf-croquet is much better than
nothing ; it provides good excuse for an hour or so in the
open when you have finished work in garden or study. The
lawn is on the little plateau that is our garden level ; quite
a fine position save for the fact that it faces east and west instead
of north and south. Then, too, the soil is sandy here and it
has been necessary to bring many barrow-loads of rich mould
from the floor of the wood. There could be no correct play
even if the grass would grow well ; cutting and rolling would

always be the best exercise available ; we know in our hearts that the turf should be taken up again and the ground levelled. We had to wait for the first attempt at lawn making until the passing and sealing of the drain pipes from cottage and bungalow, and the pipes that carry water, light and power. Only when all was complete and the sanitary inspector satisfied, could the work on the lawn go forward steadily. It was a hard job, too, for the good mould had to be carted for some distance and then spread, and grass could not be sown until the ground had settled.

Yet when we had undone the evil work of sparrows and guarded the seed and enjoyed an early game of croquet we felt proud. The lawn itself stands lightly on its sand and gravel foundation. The grass seed that was sown there is Somebody's Worst, though that was not the description in the advertisement. It is the strangest " lawn mixture " though it might have made a tolerable grazing pasture, for the grass looks not only coarse but succulent, fit for geese or for cart horses on Sunday after a hard week ; it is rich in plantain, sorrel, dandelion and creeping buttercup. Yet owing to the nature of the herbage and seed bed and the variety of levels, a thoroughly exciting and sporting game is assured, and while it is quite impossible for the expert to back his own chances, there is no occasion for the beginner to despair. The ball that is struck well and truly with the centre of the mallet may elect to describe a semi-circle, it has been known to take a hoop in its stride. So, too, may the ball that was hit with the side of the mallet, or hit too hard or not hard enough. You never know what will happen, until momentum is exhausted ; you cannot guess the goal, consequently excitement is sustained ; there is a more intense rivalry, a more definite reliance on chance than you would find round a roulette table. To ask a good tennis or cricket player to show his skill is to rouse him to anger or modesty, though normally he may be a stranger to both. Games are not fast but they are furious. Play takes a lot out of people who are not accustomed to it and several friends have given in after the first game, inventing inadequate excuses. But only one has been rude enough to say she would prefer a' game of ping-pong if we had a table handy.

15.—A Conservatory.

An advertisement in one of the country papers announced a " sectional conservatory " complete with furnace for sale at a low price, and drew me through the leafy lanes to the small holding on which its owner raises fruit, flowers and, incidentally, hopes. Mr. Mould received me in person. He is outsize, has several spare chins and apparently does not wear a coat on week days, though a spacious waistcoat had a hard struggle to contain him. I don't think he could be a lover of his fellow men ; his detachment was complete, his aloofness impressive.

Proud possessor of several conservatories, the one he had to offer must have been, I think, the first of the series ; it looked tired of life. No paint had come its way until quite recently and then the single coat had been hasty and inadequate. A few panes were cracked, the heating apparatus belonged to the palmy days of Queen Victoria, the rust that covered it as with a garment proclaimed many winters of inactivity. Mr. Mould patted the door of the conservatory with some approach to affection.

" She don't look as smart as some o' th' t'others," he admitted, " but there ain't a better owd house nowheres. Bolted, mind ye ; a child could take it to pieces."

A really harsh puff of wind might have been equally effective but I said nothing of that rude kind ; I merely grunted.

" If you was to go to a man an' want him to build ye one that size," said Mr. Mould, speaking as though he were addressing a public meeting, " he couldn't help but ast ye twenty-five pun', that might be tharty bein' everything's a-goin' up. I'm sellin' it f'r six where it stands. There's bin a gent along after it, it ain't a hour agone. He should say he'd goo back to his an' tell his wife about it. Heated an' all, mind ye." He was referring, I think, to the greenhouse, though there would have been some excuse for the gent, had he come a long way to find what awaited him. It is a curious truth that, when I consider the purchase of anything, there is someone in the background hurrying to get the bargain if I let it slide through my clumsy hands.

" The boiler's badly cracked," I remarked boldly, perhaps vulgarly, after a brief inspection.

" Couldn't help hisself," explained Mr. Mould ; " he git hot so quickly. Mos'ly bound to crack when you're a really good boiler like that."

" Some of the wood seems a bit rotten," I ventured, after further examination.

" You kin buy a bit o' deal an' put that to rights," explained Mr. Mould. " That ain't dear to-day, ain't deal."

" Door on this side seems to be warped," I urged.

" That's a good door, though I sez it," Mr. Mould assured me.

" I don't think I like the house," I said finally.

" I never thought ye did," retorted Mr. Mould. " Started findin' fault along o' her soon as ever you come. Well, there's a many what'll be on'y too glad to have her."

He dismissed me without anger or even interest, presumably there have been other visitors who do not recognise a bargain when they see one.

16.—GLASS.

A note in my Diary reminds me that this is an anniversary of the completion of the first glass house. Here is as faithful a conversational record as I can set down to tell how the conservatory and her children came into being.

The L.A. : " I don't think I could face a conservatory. Glasshouses are always ugly. I shall find myself thinking of the Crystal Palace and the great big splodges that disfigure Kew Gardens."

The Scribe : " I can never be really happy without a conservatory. I want to raise chrysanthemums and tomatoes and cinerarias and some choice fruit, melons and early strawberries particularly. The house should be a long one, sufficiently big to give you early vegetables and colour in the dark days. The cinerarias I have in mind——"

The L.A. (a little moved) : " Those things are all right if they don't get flyblown. If I forgot my dislike for glass,

THE GREENHOUSE

you wouldn't ask me to give up any of the garden? You wouldn't want to put it where I couldn't help seeing it, would you?"

The Scribe: "I thought that between the study and the wood——"

The L.A. (firmly): "Impossible. Just fancy having the view over the valley cut out by a greenhouse. You would come to hate it."

The Scribe (with resignation): "Very well. Have it where you like. But (resolutely) it must be thirty feet long, at least; I don't want a toy (prophetically). The time will come when you'll say to me, ' I'm glad we have a large green-house; it's indispensable.' "

The L.A.: "I'll go and talk to Martin (the gardener). I think if we put it up against the wood and next to the large poultry house, we could turn that into a potting shed and tool house. There might be a four-foot way between them."

The Scribe (coldly) : " You can settle all those things with him."

This is how the greenhouse entered into manifestation. In a way it had to fight for life before it was born. While the site was being levelled, a bad job this, for there were elm roots everywhere, the gardener talked delicately of " lights." His plea, which includes references to a melon pit and a couple of frames given to cucumbers, was irresistible, and the contractor weighed in with a suggestion far more sound than the greenhouse that followed. " Build your frames against the brickwork of the house," he said, " and I can leave an open space, the size of one brick, behind each and put a sliding panel in. Then, when you want to heat your frames the panel can be raised."

This was a bright idea ; ground was levelled, brick work laid, a concrete path made across the floor. The L.A. and I had been considering all manner of problems relating to gardens, but glass had not been discussed until the morning when I took her down to the conservatory. " She recalls Venus rising from the sea," I remarked mendaciously. " So beautiful, so unexpected, so radiantly responsive to the sun."

" I haven't any poetic fancies," said the L.A., " but I remember some drives through suburbs by the Thames. The grounds seemed to be full of things like that ; if they could have been cleared away those gardens would have been a delight, the flowers and trees were lovely. Aren't you glad you took my advice ? "

" When I was in Morocco," I told her, " I learned some Moorish proverbs. One was this : Always ask your wife's advice. Never take it."

" You've told me," countered the L.A., " that Morocco has ceased to be a kingdom and has become a dependency. Their indifference to women's advice didn't exactly help the Moors, did it ? "

I refused, very properly, to follow this argument, and spoke of the value of fruit grown in pots to ripen for the table several weeks before the open air varieties are available.

A little heat was indicated, and this brought us up against a further problem.   How should we heat the greenhouse ? The old and expensive method of iron pipes and a pit to hold the stove had been wiped out, or so I was assured.   There is no need to waste time in this fashion when you have power laid on.   A single point in the conservatory would heat radiators or feed an electric radiator that is said to give out heat quite effectively over a considerable area.   Then there are one or two oil plants alleged to be fool-proof and suited to the work, and the only question to be considered is the effect of various heats upon plant life.   Later, after considering all the different methods, we found the stove and pipes had most in their favour, but none can contemplate without modesty the results achieved, or regard without emotion the fashion in which a conservatory stove will deceive, disappoint and vex a gardener, how readily it will suffer from old age and decay, how expensive replacement can be, how many additional expenses stand between the purchase of a new stove and the hours of its first functioning.

CHAPTER IV

COUNTRY FOLK

17.—A VETERAN.

THE garden at the end of the far-away village through which I pass on rare occasions is not so trim and tidy as when I saw it first, though leaves have been swept from the paths, trees pruned, vegetable waste cleared. The new owner will carry on the tradition of his grandfather who first saw light when King William IV was on the throne and Queen Victoria a child in Kensington Palace. The veteran whom I knew well may have heard faint echoes of the Chartist rising and felt the benefit of the Repeal of the Corn Laws ; the revolution of 1848 must have come to him as a thrice-told tale ; he listened to the first stories of the Indian Mutiny and rumours of Zulu and Afghan wars. The South African campaign found him approaching " his seventy," and the only memory of the Great War was the crash of a Zeppelin not very far from his home. Electric light, telephones, telegrams, daily papers on sale in the village, all these things found him past his prime, wireless only came when hearing had gone. But from first to last he tended his garden after the fashion of old country-folk ; he could plant and cultivate, prune and bud with hands from which the years might steal strength but not skill. When actually in his hundred and first year, he dug potatoes, but with winter he retired to his bedroom, though not at first to his bed ; he sat by an open window overlooking with dim eyes the space he had cultivated so long. Kind folk called upon him, bearing little gifts ; their tributes pleased and surprised him ; he did not know his own age and the parish register was needed to confirm local belief. Quite recently Father Time visited the village ; he responded to the quiet call. The wooden cross in the village churchyard is very new, it looks unsuited for a memorial of one who dwelt so long in the land. For a time the garden remained worthy of its old master, then I noted a change and, chatting with new tenant's wife, I suggested that her husband didn't have quite as much free time as his grandfather.

"Grandad," she replied a little scornfully, "tore hisself out over the garden, but I shouldn't like my Bill to work like that. Time he's done his day's job I like him to come to th' Hall, or listen to a band o' music on th' wireless, not to go muddlin' about the garden till he can't hardly see. That kind of thing was all right for the old folk; they'd nothing else to do."

"I suppose," I said gently, "that you never cared for gardening?"

"I've never took much notice of it," she replied, "except of course I want Bill to grow veg'tables f'r th' house, an' I like a few flowers whiles, to put in a vorze. But if I got time to spare I'd liefer take the bus an' goo to the pichers than set in a garden, like me gran'mother used. I don't know what she found to see in it, poor old thing, except it was that Grandad tended it. They didn't care much for anybody 'cept each other."

18.—Mr. Tripp.

In one part that I visited soon after coming here there is a thriving village hall and, less than a mile away a thatched cottage that houses Mr. Tripp, freeholder, pensioner, gardener, man of independent views; he takes an angry interest in me. We soon became unfriendly friends. He should have been educated; the face that his fierce little eyes brighten is refined, the forehead high, the lips thin, the chin well-formed. He lives in his garden when weather permits and holds passers in watchful suspicious regard. Mr. Tripp nodded tolerantly and spoke civilly enough when we met first, but has waxed critical since. Now when I pass his garden he never fails to challenge conversation. I remember asking him if he went much to the Parish Hall in the nearby village; it had been established for several years past. "I ain't never been an' I ain't never goin'," he replied firmly.

I looked my query and he answered it.

"Too much gadding about nowadays," he explained. "I don't howd with it. We didn't have such things when I was young and we never felt the miss of them. You want to keep yourself to yourself come the rough weather; you don't want to traipse here, there an' everywhere. You go out in the dark and the first old motor car to come along 'll knock you down and kill you, soon as look at you ; they come whizzin' past every hour o' th' day and night, drat 'em."

" Young people need these clubs——" I began.

" Never mind them," cried Mr. Tripp. " I shan't never be young no more, an' you won't neither. Too much o' this dancin' an' too much cards. If I'd towd me father I was goin' out dancin', he'd ha' clouted me."

" A little harsh, your father ? " I queried.

" Father lived respectable," protested Mr. Tripp. " Come the summer he worked in the garden, an' come the winter he set by th' fire. Lived to his eighty-one but nobody ever saw him dance, nor yet play cards, nor yet go gallavantin', 'sted o' minding his business. If I had me way, I'd shut the Hall up an' keep folk out o' mischief. They'd thank me f'r it, time they're old enough. You can't tend y'r garden, time you're settin' in a Hall," he added, " an' that's no use pertending you can."

" But on cold dark evenings ? "

" Me own fire's warmest," said Mr. Tripp decisively. " If a man got a fire th' least he kin do is to sit by it."

19.—AN ELDER.

One elderly farm worker who had done odd jobs for me was taken ill at the end of September and I went to see him. There was no recovery for him and he knew it.

I expressed the usual conventional hope that I'd see him in my garden when the spring came round. He shook his head.

" I'll be under nex' year's daisies," he said, " but there, that don't sin'ify. I've had me harvest supper, and took me harvest money, an' th' owd overseer won't be able to turn me outer house an' home."

In other words he was happy because he would not be sent to the union to die. It was not death that the old folk feared, it was the stigma of the work-house.

THE SHIRE HORSE

20.—THE VILLAGE BLACKSMITH.

On a visit to a friend whose place is a few miles away, I stopped to speak to Mr. Coyle, blacksmith and handyman. An old gossip of mine and oracle of the " Dog and Duck," he kindly explained why winter returns annually. You can always learn from Mr. Coyle if you have humility.

A big shire horse had been led away, complete with four new shoes ; the wise man had leisure.

" That's two coats cowder than it was last week," he began ; " an' all along of the winter. A man," continued Mr. Coyle, "wants to wrop himself up every time he come out of the warm. If he does that, he won't catch no chills, that's likely."

I nodded agreement.

" There's some what grumbles about the winter," continued Mr. Coyle. " We were talking about it in the Dog only last night. They couldn't understand it, but I set 'em right. ' Time you've done your job of work,' I told 'em, ' you wanter go to sleep, an' that the same thing with the arth. You've had your vegebles an' your fruit an' your corn an' now the sun want a rest an' th' arth want a rest an' when things stop work they get cold.' They couldn't all see it, but some on 'em could."

" That's a great idea," I admitted. " How did you come by it ? "

" I've looked inter things," explained Mr. Coyle. " If I put me bellows down, me fire will go out ; if I set still 'stead o' moving, I get cold. When the arth stop working an' th' sun's up late an' down early, everything get cold."

" Nothing could be simpler," I admitted.

" Come the spring," continued Mr. Coyle, " the sun'll get up to time an' th' land'll git busy an' we shan't feel th' cold any more ; we shan't be able to ; that'll be warm."

" Did you tell your friends that ? " I asked him, and he nodded.

" When things puzzle 'em they ast me," he went on seriously, " an' I start to think. I get a lot o' time for thinking nowadays," he added, a little ruefully. " When I was young you didn't have much chance ; one horse arter the other, all the livelong day. But there ain't half the horses there were, ne yet a quarter. There's some folk don't give no heed to thinking," he continued solemnly, " but I always say that if we thought more, there wouldn't be so many mistakes in the world. If you do a thing without thinking," concluded the Oracle, " you're just as likely to be wrong as you are to be right, an' more."

I thanked Mr. Coyle and expressed the entire agreement looked for. He is a large, fat man, heavy, bald and scant of breath but rich in assurance. Many of the words he utters have capital letters. There is something in him that reminds me of Mr. Willett, landlord of the Maypole Inn that Barnaby Rudge knew. He can suffer anything but contradiction ; if asked to edit the " Times " or command the Home Fleet he would take off his coat, moisten his hands in fashion I can only regard as unpleasant and set to work, calling upon all men to see for themselves how such tasks should be approached. In the village they will tell you that Master Coyle got a fine brain and that it profits no man to argyfy with him ; he is at most respected where men dip great thoughts in beer. If you have a new problem to face, send for Mr. Coyle ; he will offer to solve it out of hand. He has even been known to succeed. He can recall many cases of which he is the sole surviving witness.

21.—TOUCHING MR. MATT.

As you travel down the road that stretches from London through Essex and Suffolk into Norfolk you may pass a signpost which does not say " Merrywind three miles," but something rather like it.

I don't give you the proper name of the village, because if I did there might be requests for detail, and these I can't supply. You see, as the traveller passes through a country-side that still retains the fashions of an earlier age, he finds a few truly Victorian folk. They are very precious ; he likes to keep them to himself, lest they be spoilt by too much inspection. They can recall the Crimean War, not because they took part in it but because their fathers told them how the price of corn rose ; they can remember the bad harvest of 1879 because their own wages started on a long decline. They have never been to the place they call " Lunnon "—they have never used the telephone, they would be far too self-conscious. No motor omnibus or " sharrybang " disturbs their repose. They hear of progress in varied forms, and mistrust it heartily ; they wonder audibly and a little angrily what this here world's a-comin' to ! They are folk whose company I seek.

The grand-daughter of a man who belongs to this pleasant past gave us tea on our way from town. We sat in the garden of an oak and elm framed cottage with deep red tiles on which the house-leek grows ; the belief in its virtues is age-old, going back to Pagan times. Apart from the cottage and its house-leek on the tiles, Mr. Matt arrests attention—he has a resolute chin, blue eyes and a shock of grey hair ; obviously the master of his small domain accustomed to bear rule if only over a few square yards.

In the next village only a couple of miles away, a few Council houses are being built, to the deep annoyance of Mr. Matt, who demanded to be told why the Council come interferin' what don't concern it. I temporised, but my host was in earnest, he demanded acquiescence and sympathy. Here is our conversation.

Mr. Matt (as his grand-daughter reached the table by the side of the bed he was weeding, with a dish of excellent scones, hot and buttered): " They've come fresh out of me oven. Me grand-daughter's a master. I larnt her to bake. But the Council housen! Did you ever hear the like? Sech interferences! I never did! "

The Scribe (cautiously): " Are they very bad? Have you seen them? "

Mr. Matt (sharply): " Tain't likely I'd hobble two miles, my time o' life, to see sech contraptions. When I was a lad we got twenty or tharty cottages about, and they all bin pulled down or fallen down. There you are. Pull down one lot and set up another. Nonsense to my thinkin'. It's a marcy they never done it here."

The Scribe: " I met an old lady a month or two ago who told me that if I wanted a cottage at any time, to go to the Council."

Mr. Matt (scornfully): " An' have everybody a-top o' ye, an' everybody pryin' into ye all day long, so that you don't belong to yourself no more than th' pump on the green. Better goo to th' workhouse an' have done with it. There you got to acquaint with everybody."

The Scribe: " People don't mind company these days. The Village Clubs——"

Mr. Matt: " My owd father never went to no Club."

The Scribe: " There weren't any in your father's time."

Mr. Matt: " An' a good job, too. He never missed 'em, I be bound. Time he came from work he tended his garden."

The Scribe: " People get about more now-a-days; they like company."

Mr. Matt: " More shame for 'em. I don't. I've never bin fudderer than —— "—he named the village with the Council houses—" in all me born days, an' I've never ailed anything, an' got every tooth in me head. An' there's owd Bob Patten across th' green, lived in Lunnon nigh sevin year, an' they took his apprentix out afore he come back here. If he hadn't gone gadding about, the doctor folk couldn't ha' caught him. They didn't do things like that in my young days. You kep' what you got."

I have concealed names but the opinions are recorded faithfully. I think that Mr. Matt is an exception to the general rule. Most of the country folk, particularly the softer sex, prefer the new and the minority consists of very aged folk who have never been in touch with latter-day progress. I thought I would have a last word. Here it is :

The Scribe : " Do you have a wireless ? "

Mr. Matt : " 'Tain't likely. I don't want all manner o' folk I've never met in all me life comin' into me room an' talking to me. If th' folk wanter come to mine they got to wait till I ast 'em. I don't mind the band o' music now an' agen. Blacksmith, up street, bin an' made it play to me whiles, but that ain't all it should be always, nit by no means. And I don't want 'em talkin' to me. Why, there was one or two on 'em wanted to larn me gardenin'—I lay I kep' a garden gooin' time they was a baby in arms. Imperence ! "

Perhaps the B.B.C. will take note.

I should say that Mr. Matt's grand-daughter served an excellent tea, with hot scones and jam and watercress, charged eighteen pence, and took her tip with a curtsey that was none the less attractive because it belonged to the age when crinolines were worn and ankles were unheard of. I have no doubt but that the old gentleman oppresses and represses her severely and with the very best intentions in the world, but what can you or I do about it ? Mr. Matt was born to bear rule.

22.—MASTERLY MR. MOLE.

In years long past Mr. Jonathan Mole did odd jobs for me. He was a blue-eyed phlegmatic man, whose paces suggested that he was by birth and intention a snail. Certainly he did scant justice to the livelier little creature whose name he had assumed. Offered another job he left the district. But

quite recently in a remote hamlet I called at the village shop
and, to my surprise, found Mrs. Mole. We chatted. Mr.
Mole's bachelor brother had died and left him the business ;
he had come from the other side of the county to take charge.

"But I don't see him," I remarked, glancing round, and
Mrs. Mole explained.

"Mr. Mole doesn't like himself in the shop," she explained,
sotto voce ; "folk round here are so strange. They'll ask
for one thing from behind one counter and another from
t'other. He says he never knows what people want next,
and that aggravates him ; he should say that's what they do it
for. Then, too, his brother kep' a list of everything he
ordered and what it cost and what he looked to make on't;
and them figures worrit Mr. Mole. His brain's too big for
such tiffling things. He wanted to sell th' shop but nobody
come along to buy it, so I up an' said I'd try me hand."

"How are you getting on ? " I enquired, as I paid for a
trifling purchase.

"I manage all right," said Mrs. Mole, confidently, " but
there, you see, I never was like Mr. Mole. He's got a dreadfully active brain. There isn't a shop could hold it, except
that was in Lunnon or some such place. He potters about
the garden and reads the paper and listens to the wireless."

"And you do, the rest of the work and look after the
house ? " I suggested.

"That's easy enough for me," explained Mrs. Mole. " I
haven't any head to speak about, leastways not f'r big things.
He's got a wonderful brain, has Mr. Mole. He can talk
about anything large ; his mind's too full to take in shops
and such. But give him big things and he's all right—
Europe an' Asia an' America, an' such places. An' war an'
peace an' trade an' prices, an' a League o' somethin' or other,
I mis' remember what. That's a treat to hear all about sech
things ; I can't keep up with him. So I jus' look arter
the shop, an' I bin an' brought it round nicely. I don't think
Mr. Mole'll sell it arter all."

CHAPTER V

WINTER COMES AND GOES

23.—Winter Looks In.

Winter is a word of no pleasing significance but I think that some of us, the writer among them, do the season less than justice. The reflection was forced upon me this afternoon when I paused for a few minutes to see what was lighting the world outside my study window. It was a sunset, all gold, shining above a valley along which the first mists of evening gathered.

Behind the hill that shuts out our brief view, a column of smoke was rising vertically in the windless air, some hedge trimmer or woodman had made a fire, and was burning much that with proper treatment might have been turned into sound compost. On the suet suspended from elm branches beyond the reach of their enemies, three little tom-tits were taking a happy meal, on another piece the robin who is never far away from us perched triumphantly. Down the hill in one of the runs, chickens were gathered round the gardener, by the wood the carpenter was repairing the gate that gives direct access to the shelter of evergreens. Across the meadow a giant oak tree stood up, gaunt yet beautiful, the delicate tracery of branches revealed as never when all the world is green. A flock of wild pigeons was streaming across to sleep in the wood. On the red-berried thorn before my study window, blackbirds were feeding.

As I watched, the sun sank out of sight but contrived to fire the clouds so radiantly that birds flying between me and the light appeared faintly illumined as they passed where the scarlet background glowed. Pheasants called good-night, far below me a barn owl wheeled past the alders.

Inside, the fire was bright on the hearth; some excellent music was on its way—and to make life more complete, more self-contained, the telephone had broken down.

24.—ECHOES OF MORNING.

" The Winter is over and gone." This is a line I like to repeat on all occasions after December 21st has brought the shortest day to any year. I know it is merely an expression of hope, an exercise of the kind advocated by the late Dr. Coué ; February may yet fill the dykes and March blow tiles off the roof, but I refuse to allow these facts to prejudice me. The sun rises shortly before eight and goes off duty at half-past four, but we are no longer ice-bound and morning papers are arriving regularly. During the worst weather the postman, old but resolute, brought letters to time, only newspapers were a movable feast. At a season when there had been question of rights of way, two gates were closed for a while, and as the papers' schoolboy guardian could not cycle by the woodside, he left his master's wares at the village forge in charge of Providence and the blacksmith. Few could give that engaging lad any lesson in finding lines of least resistance. When gates were opened he had acquired the forge habit ; it was hard to relinquish. Then came ice and snow, and apparently the daily press will not travel in such company at sunrise. The period of readjustment was slow, there were mornings when hope told a flattering tale only to die when the flattery became apparent.

To-day open gates and open weather, early sunrise and awakening birds all unite in pointing to better times coming. The papers find way to the breakfast table, and I am able to assure the L.A. that as I am only glancing at the front page of the one and the middle page of the other, the whole survey will not take a moment. She pretends to certain doubts but they are never justified, unless the news is of a kind that demands a little concentration from all who take an intelligent interest in the world's progress. I am careful to explain all this—a few minutes later.

The newspaper habit is almost universal but there are a few people who content themselves with a sensational Sunday journal. I asked an old countryman how he came to make his choice.

" I like to read about what they bin doin' in that owd Lunnon o' yourn," he told me, " an' what th' owd judge said to 'em. Most all th' bad uns in my paper come from Lunnon an' th' rest of 'em come from the sheers.   Bad owd places each o' th' both o' 'em."

The sheers or shires are an object of contempt in the eyes of men of Essex and East Anglia, and the belief that I own Lunnon has been held by several elderly farmworkers of my acquaintance, at least they were of my acquaintance, but have passed out of reach now.   I have known men and women who never saw a train, never read a newspaper, never heard a gramophone, who died before the aeroplane or the wireless came along.   But to all outward seeming their lives were filled, though they asked for little more than enough to eat, a fire in the grate, and an occasional glass of beer with a sing-song in their favourite house of call.   From their ranks came those who always spoke to me of " that Lunnon o' yourn," as if they knew it for a worthless possession in untrustworthy hands.

25.—THE PLOUGHMAN.

I had talked awhile with a ploughman a week earlier on a nearby farm where he was working on a heavy-land field. The morning was full of sunshine.

" You need warm days like this for tractor work in winter," I suggested.   He had checked the machine at the end of a furrow to oil a bearing.

" Yes," he replied, " the old horse-plough kept ye warm, these things freeze ye, time that's cowd.   I don't howd with 'em an' that's th' truth, but I gotter allow they get over the ground."

" You've plenty of company," I remarked, pointing to the gulls and rooks.

" They don't like themselves neither," he said in a whisper, as though he would not like them to hear him betray their confidence.   " A tractor goos too fast for 'em.   They're used to the horse plough ; it gives them time to pick up everything. They can't stop to hunt a furrow properly behind a tractor. Every bird's afraid the others'll get ahead of him.   It's a scramble, is a tractor.   They'd liefer have the horses back. I know it, and so would I if you was to ask me to tell ye th' truth.   But there, rooks an' gulls is company, time you haven't a horse to talk to."

GULLS

26.—A Sunday Walk in Marshland.

One morning, a Sunday, we took a walk in the sunshine to enjoy, among lanes and fields, the peace of the world. There was no wind, the grey leafless poplars could stand rigidly to attention. A morning frost had just passed from some well-ploughed arable, clods shone in the light as though they had been burnished. Plover, gulls, rooks floated lazily over the land or hunted furrows ; only when they are clearing up grubs are gulls useful to man. Half a dozen curlew fed by the water, their long, curved, questing bills raked the mud ; in intervals of their search they made winter music. They have other calls for spring, when they frequent northern moors and sing to a small family of straight-billed nestlings. In the late autumn and winter they change home, vary diet and rely upon a strange disfigurement to enable them to probe for worms and the small life of fleet and ditch.

Robin called gently from a holly bush, blackbird boldly from hedgerow oak. The peace of sabbath was on the farm of the burnished clods. Through an open door of the steading we could see half a dozen plough horses in their stalls, steadily munching the hay piled into racks above ; it must have been well made and stacked dry, fragrance of summer fields still lingered. Their easy chains clanked as they lifted mild eyes to the intruders. Even cows chewed the cud as though they felt that a day had been given to make milk at leisure ; folded sheep on the last of the kale were equally aware. Here and there on our walk we met pairing partridges. Coveys had broken up. I think all wild life knew that the shooting season was over. Already the pheasants' colouring seemed more brilliant than before, buck hares were beginning their scampering fights, plover courting. Fear had passed ; some foreknowledge of the joyous season brings back courage to the countless little lives we persecute in such dull, unimaginative fashion.

27.—ROOKS AND OTHERS.

Before the first snowdrop was out, in the first year of our sojourn, I heard rooks courting in a neighbour's grounds ; they were inspecting old homes in the tree tops, inspecting and testing, for when an elm passes from health the topmost branches are first to tell the tale. They stiffen and grow brittle ; rooks having tried them as they never fail to do, change their address. It may be too early for building or even for repair work, but it is not too soon nor too cold for courtship. Perhaps in the far distance of the clear afternoons they can see the hosts of Spring gathering for the invasion that all the world welcomes ; in January you never pause to remember how cold, dismal and wet April days can be. Rooks are the most self-centred of birds. Friends tell me that in Lowestoft during the last war they pursued their lawful occasions while German shells were dropping round them ; nightingales, by the way, are nearly as indifferent to noise. On this January afternoon when the sun had set behind the wood, sending a long crimson glow through the bare branches and the day's work was ending, I heard a thrush,

ROOKS

defying wind and weather. He sang with feathers puffed
out as though to keep himself warm, and I remembered
suddenly how, many years ago, Thomas Hardy, listening to
one that flung a like challenge to a winter's night, wrote
certain delightful verses ending:

> " . . . . *I could think there trembled through*
> *His happy good-night air*
> *Some blessed Hope, whereof he knew*
> *And I was unaware.*"

There the wisest and most lovable of our countrymen touched
a note to which some among us may, in our dull uncertain
fashion, vibrate gratefully. On dim, dark days, a burst of
sunshine that makes cock pheasants call from the wood,
or tempts the song thrush to forget for a moment that
February still looms across the horizon; a sunrise and

sunsetting, clear and serene over an empty world, suffice to fill us with vain but pleasant thoughts that the march of the year must respond to our desires, rather than to laws we neither understand nor control.

28.—FEBRUARY'S BIRD.

On a still morning, sitting by the side of the wood in the shelter of the summerhouse, I heard the song of the gold-crest and marked two of these exquisite little birds at play among the fir tree tops.   I think one should expect the gold crest to come into song now but that song is very delicate ; pitched high it is hard to catch.   If several other birds are singing the note passes me ; only if I am in the right position to hear and the breeze is light and favourable can the notes be captured.   Often I have watched these tiny visitors playing among the high branches of the Scotch firs, and have known quite well that they have been in song and that the song was not for me to hear.

One of the handsome mistle thrushes that haunts the garden has decided that nesting time is at hand ; he has started to build in a fork of the high ash branches just as though hail and snow were things of the past and March would forget to come in like a lion.   A blackbird was equally foolish last year, and before the nest could hold eggs it was half filled with snow.   Robins are pairing already, the male birds in shining nuptial plumage, their ladies look shabby by their side.   We have at least three pairs here, one by the wood, one in the garden, another down by the stream.   I have spread food for all and sundry, the tit mice will fly together to the coconuts, a mixed multitude will gather to the food tray.   But I have yet to find two robins feeding in company.

Pheasants come down to the spring to drink.   I stood on the road to watch three or four scraping leaves at the edge of a wood, a few miles from home.

" Clent themselves up wonderful," remarked my friend the hedger, as he straightened his back.   " An' when they're a few weeks older they'll be fightin' one another for the owd hens.   You'd think they'd had enough trouble with the guns without looking for any more.   But there, I suppose they take

GOLDCREST

arter men. When they towd me to go out furrin' and kill Jarmans, I didn't know why they wanted I should. Jarmans ha'n't done no hurt to me, nor yet me to them." He turned to give a fresh edge to his hook.

"This here's a rum world; that don't matter if you're a man or a pheasant seem'ly, you can't keep off quarrelling."

29.—WINTER AGAIN.

A gale from the south-west is hurling iced rain against the cottage, wind has found weak points that the builders over-looked—in doors and window frames. Roads and lanes are deserted, no wise man leaves his own fireside. Winter has returned as a harsh conqueror; you can hear the trees of the woodland moaning, as his legions invade their sanctuary. There is but one consolation to be won from the brief, necessary struggle for exercise; it comes in the moment when wet wrappings are thrown aside, when slippers have replaced heavy boots, and an armchair by the fire calls for no more than choice of a favourite book.

What a pity it is that we cannot hibernate; if I had so many to dispose of I would gladly give up ten winters for five summers, and welcome the exchange. The next best thing is perhaps to sit by the fire and recall or anticipate the gracious seasons, as the Wizard did in the " Earthly Paradise." And it may be that during a brief lull in the storm, the gardener will bring pots of flowering blooms to cheer the eye and remind us of good times coming. If they cannot altogether fill the empty spaces, or if the eyes tire of the printed page, one has but to touch a switch and from some distant centre music, or news of a far-away world will fill the room. All the clever men and women in the world are queued up behind the microphone, waiting to deliver their message. They don't know you or me, but if we listen to what they have to say or play or sing to us and we are grateful and appreciative, their task is complete. Winter can work many woes but it cannot keep friendly voices and beautiful music from riding the hurricane and reaching the study on this remote hillside.

The other night or rather in the early morning, I woke to a rare sound, the cry of wild geese. There is nothing quite like the appeal to the ears of the lover of bird life. You know the geese will be flying high up, head to wind, in their own formation, the shape of the letter V; that they are winging their way to some desolate place where none can follow. I have only heard them calling when winter has gripped the land, and always in the night hours.

I spoke of hibernation to Mr. Tripp.

" You don't wanter come along with a mouthful o' long words nobody ain't ever heerd on," he said sharply. So I made due apology and became more explicit.

" That's what all sensible folk do, 'cept they come from furrin' parts," he agreed, a little sourly. " Time a man ain't young no longer, he wanter set by his fire come th' winter arternoon an' he wanter goo to bed right early. That's what th' sun doe⸚, an' you can't goo amiss if you do th' same.

" Me father never went out arter November," he continued, " an' not much then. He got his fruit, an' honey, an' veg'ables indoors, an' his firin'. He'd worked all the spring an' summer an' autumn an' he worn't goin' to take cowd or rheumatiz along o' wet feet, 'tweren't likely. He set in th' ingle-nook an' slep' when he wanted to. An' one day," concluded Mr. Tripp thoughtfully, " time he wore in his eighty

odd he never woke up. Went off dead like," he added.
"Doctor should ha' said his heart bin stopped beatin'. Hearts
are rum things to my thinkin'. He never ailed anything an'
yet his heart ouldn't goo on."

30.—COLOUR OF GREY DAYS.

We have no reason to believe that flowers, born out of
their due time, know anything about perils that attend their
place in the vanguard of spring. Theirs is a post of honour
and danger, similar to that taken by army leaders in days when
hand-to-hand fighting was the decisive factor in battles.
Before Agincourt, Shakespeare presents the Duke of York
saying to the King :

"My Lord, most humbly on my knee I beg the leading
of the vaward." King Henry replies, "Take it, brave
York," and the Duke goes contented to his death.

Every year when winter is waning, countless little flowers
ask the Lord of Light that they may lead the vaward and
merrily they lead it, too, until the sun sets and the frost steals
from river level and the harsh east passes over their maiden
rows. Nor are flowers the only sufferers ; the earliest
thrush and blackbird may find their nests destroyed. But
in spite of tragedy there is gay life or colouring even in late
February, orange of lichens on old trunks in the wood, bright
green of moss, gold of gorse and dandelion, virgin white
of snowdrop, flame of first celandine and anemone. Ivy
strands that I plucked and planted several years ago show new
life and gay greenery ; they hide the nakedness of walls.
Colour, however faintly rising, is the key-note of life just now,
the rusty tints of winter and decay are passing slowly, too
slowly for those of us who would like to see fresh hedgerows
and wakening trees weeks or months before Nature's
appointed hour. But to watch what may be seen to-day and
to think of official summer time with its sunny hours and
singing birds as an unopened treasure house, is to feel rich.
Nothing has been taken from the year's gifts and, weather
permitting, England has the finest summer in the world.
At least, I think so, after much experience of summer in other
lands.

I found an old-age pensioner of my acquaintance walking down his narrow garden path to the bank where the gorse bloomed.

" I allus come out to have a look at it this time o' year," he explained. " That doos me good when I got nothin' in me garden. Bright things are help f'r y'r eyes," he went on, " leastaways I count they're good f'r mine. I've allus looked f'r bright flowers an' I ain't never ailed anything about me eyes, so I count flowers must be what they want."

31.—SIGNS OF SPRING.

How the year moves towards the spring ! Already the sun starts his work before half-past seven and does not go home until after five, nearly ten hours of gracious activity that calls to willow catkins and honeysuckle leaves in warm corners and encourages shy violets to grace garden ways that else were wellnigh bare. And, given just a little space of clear sky for light to shine in, birds make instant response and you may even hear the skylark for the first time in the year, a song-thrush when the world is hushed for sunsetting and, at other times, blackbird or stormcock.

Life rises in the hedgerows. Nature has no regulations to check overcrowding there, nearly everything seen is but a pale reflection of what it might be. The L.A. and I returned after the " tradesmen " had gone their ways, to a very old practice. We went out in February and dug up roots of hedgerow plants that were showing green leaves ; they could not be too common. Wild parsley, *arum maculatum*, stitchwort, violet, celandine, primrose, dandelion, archangel, a dozen or a score of these roots were housed in bowls and brought in beyond reach of the harsh east wind. We could draw April to our tables before March had started on her rough journey to the equinox ; our plants, free for once from overcrowded hedgerow, grew so well that their old time companions might not have recognised them.

Prominent among them was the dandelion, that unregarded beauty " fringing the dusty way with harmless gold," and the lesser celandine for which Wordsworth had equal love. To understand how much goes to waste on every side when winter leaves us, you need no more than a bowl or two of the simplest growth that banks and hedgerows yield. When the time of their flowering is over, we put roots back in the nearest bank; by then the claims of the garden upon every bowl are insistent. You can cultivate dandelions until they are larger than marigolds and the young leaves make an excellent salad at a time when forced lettuces have scant flavour.

32.—A Prescription.

"Winter bin an' broke her back, an' sarve her right," said Mr. Tripp, complacently, as he suspended digging operations for a moment, to pass me the time of day.

"It is such a wonderful morning that I couldn't work," I admitted.

"Time I got a wunnerful mornin'," retorted Mr. Tripp acidly, "I like to do a mite o' work. Anybody kin sit indoors, time that rains. If you don't dig in the dry, you won't never dig in the wet."

"A walk seems the best thing for a day like this," I insisted.

"There ain't nought amiss along of a walk, if a man ain't anything better to do," he admitted. "Four miles out an' a pint of beer, and four miles home. That wants most three hours; a man don't want to swallow beer same as that was water. A pint wants to be as long as a pipe an' a pipe wants to be as long as a pint. There's some like a mossel o' bread an' cheese along of their beer," continued Mr. Tripp, reflectively, "an' I don't blame them. They all go together, by the good rights. A man wants a sunny day an' a sunny day wants a glass o' beer."

I walked on into the sunshine through a world of green things beginning to grow. I heard the bird songs of the early year and exchanged greetings with men working on the land, while musing on a world from which winter has passed. On a friendly stone by a garden gate a little girl was threading primroses into a necklace, only a child could do such a monstrous thing without offence. Small patches of spring flowers made gardens gay, there was a curious sense of elation about the countryside that was shared by man and beast, bird and flower. The famous verse from the Canticle came back to me. " For lo, the spring has come, the winter is over and gone." And I was very pleased about it.

That was yesterday. You might strain your eyesight looking for so much as a glint of sunshine to-day ; the south-west wind has brought a cold rain to bear it company. March at its worst has followed March at its best, but the memory of yesterday is still smiling happily, though there is more pleasure in an armchair by the fireside than you could find in any lane or by-way throughout the county. Even Mr. Tripp would admit as much.

A MARSHLAND SCENE.

CHAPTER VI

HERE AND THERE

33.—A Duck Decoy.

"This morning is too lovely for work, indoors or out," said the L.A. "Let us go to the marshes and lunch near the old decoy. If you miss a day like this," she went on severely, "when evening comes you'll say you're sorry and ask me why I didn't persuade you."

I surrendered at discretion. In an hour and a half we had reached our goal.

"Gooin' down to the owd 'Coy agen?" enquired the ploughman, who was finishing his bread and cheese under the hedge. It was not his dinner, it was what is called in marshland "levens" or "levenses," and is the little meal that enables him to carry on till his acre is ploughed and he goes home to dinner. He was a tall, bearded man of a type you meet in these parts. The Danes went up to Maldon more than a thousand years ago, and where they passed you can still find upstanding yellow-haired men and women.

"Yes," I told him, "to have a look round. I used to come down here long ago when it was working."

"That's tore out now," said the ploughman. "You don't wanter goo traipsin across th' meddies arter it no more. Telly f'r why; it ain't there, rightly speakin. An' there on't be nawthin' about here afore we're much owder."

"How's that?" I asked.

"Airyplines," he answered gravely. "They should say Gover'ment want forever o' airyplines round about. You can't have airyplines an' 'Coys. Telly f'r why. Time th' owd birds hear them airyplines, they goo back where they belong. That Master Sewell wouldn't have had ye fire a gun within a mile o' his 'Coy, an' now an airypline kin come over often as it likes. That's agin Natur' to my thinkin'."

"Have you seen them?" I asked him.

"Aye," he answered. "I've seed 'em many's the time, an' I don't think nawthen to 'em. Gre't noisy things to my thinkin'. You don't wanter fly. If the dear Lord bin an' wanted folk to fly, he'd ha' give 'em wings. If anybody'd pay me to goo up in one o' them contraptions I ouldn't do it. There's a lot o' folk hereabout dedn't want them comin' spoilin' th' owd 'Coy yonder, but they never took no heed o' that." He paused to take a little refreshment, probably cold tea from a tin can and wiped his mouth with the back of his hand.

"There," he said, "I must get back to me harses. If me owd father see one o' them airyplines gooin' about he ouldn't h' believed it. But there worn't a better shepherd in these parts, though I sez it. Mark my words. Time they're tired o' playin' about in the sky they'll want to get back to a 'Coy with a few ducks in it come the winter. But there won't be any."

So saying he moved off with swinging stride to where his three-horse team was waiting. There are not many plough-men who will talk so freely to a stranger; he may have known me in days when I was often at the decoy, or the compulsory silence that rings his working day may have tempted him to make a very unusual concession to a "furriner."

The marshland, with two decoys, one that may be passing and one that has passed, is perhaps the loneliest in all England.

Since corn prices crashed in 1879 it has never succeeded in recalling the great company of ploughmen and harvesters who, contented if not prosperous, filled waste places with fruits of the earth and dwelt in cottages of which scarcely a trace remains. To-day grass rules. There are sheep with here and there a grey, weatherwise shepherd of an older time, but because of heavy rains and late season, ewes and lambs had been taken to the uplands. At other times than this, " over the meadows that blossom and wither, rings but the note of a seabird's song."

May morning, dressed in sunshine, had the greening marsh to herself. Midway between the farthest farm and the sea-wall lie the remains of one decoy, pipes choked, central pond covered with rushes, all water-courses that served for drainage silted up ; yet it was here that Spring held carnival. High in the blue her larks were singing as they never sing at any other season ; over marsh fields and sea-wall boundary sand-pipers, ox-birds and redshanks with a few dunlins and wigeon wheeled in unending love flight, filling the waste with their shrill call.

Past the broken gate of the decoy, May's prodigality stood revealed. There was a bewildering odour coming from a carpet of white violets that must have been about twenty feet square. Any gardener, any garden-lover would have been proud to raise such a harvest under glass or in shelter of a south wall ; here it stood with never an admirer, two early butterflies excepted, until we came that way. There were primroses, great fat, late luscious flowers in scattered clumps, elder had broken into greenery, honeysuckle had started her summer adventure. Blackthorn was green and whitethorn red ; from an ash tree top, a chiff-chaff clamoured for recognition ; from a bush a greenfinch sang. The passion of sea-wall and saltings where the air was musical for miles had invaded the sanctuary ; spring was calling every bird and bud, every leaf and flower to fulfil its destiny.

From the pond, three couples of wild duck rose, to fly in diminishing circles round and round trees that ring the pond and then drop back in quiet water somewhere near their nests. Doe-rabbits moved contentedly across open spaces, their young families in attendance. Early bumble bees took flight. From the edge of wonderland I looked across the country and saw only half a dozen ewes in a near field, a few cattle grazing in a far one. There was no rising corn. There were no fallows waiting for ploughs, no sign of the life that ruled in days when men took seventy bushels of wheat from an acre of marvellously fertile land won from the sea ; all that prosperity had fled. But Nature then re-asserted herself. It seemed as though she had decided that, since man cannot turn her gifts to account, she would restore its pristine beauty to the land and hold high festival with two of the humblest of her lovers for an audience. To this end she had summoned to that lonely spot the most beautiful sights and sounds and scents of spring time.

For years I have gone in pursuit of Spring at her truest and best ; she has stood revealed in unexpected places, but never in fairer guise than she did between marsh, farm and sea-wall where the ruinous decoy still tells its story of times that will not return. We returned home in the late afternoon with the thought that our lines were cast in pleasant places, and we left the land that has become desolate to a silence that might well go unbroken until we return.

34.—A Country Church.

The church, with its square ivied tower and screen of trees, stands rather aloof from the public way as though in quest of repose that even a country by-way might mar. An old bearded man with a scythe was cutting the broad grass border between lychgate and porch. He might have been Father Time who had laid aside his hour-glass to do a more pleasant piece of work.

High trees and old, undulating pasture, a very restful God's acre ; everywhere the note of quietude. The morning was young but the church door was already open ; birds were greeting the sunshine ; over mounds of green earth the grass was young and vivid.

Parts of the church had stood there when Norman and Saxon met at Senlac, the tide of faith and worship might have suffered ebb and flow but " a thousand years . . . are as a watch in the night."

On the walls are memorials to worthies who did their duty and went their way, long before you and I saw the light, tributes to certain men who were just and dutiful landlords, to others who were brave soldiers, to some who lived the alloted span and others whose fulfilment came even before the middle years.   Had they found the peace that brooded over the empty church ?   Were they able to express, in some fashion more effective than mere speech, the futility of haste, anxiety and the aims that hold the lives of most of us ?

I cannot answer my own question but at least all the petty worries and fatigue of some strenuous days passed like a burden lifted suddenly in this quiet house where Time and Eternity met.

The emotions of many generations, joy and sorrow, hope and resignation had found expression here and yet the sense of tranquillity was dominant as though the end of all things is peace.   Years have passed along but at the season when full-fledged spring is preparing the way for even more delightful days, the little church comes back to me with a vision of primrose, wood sorrel and lady fern in its garden of graves.

There are hundreds of these half-forgotten houses of worship in East Anglia and elsewhere, each in its way a sanctuary.   It is sad to think that from Sunday to Sunday they stand wellnigh deserted, the undefinable gift they offer to every passer rejected and despised.

35.—THE HERONRY.

I have stolen a fine day to travel across country and visit the poor remains of a once prosperous heronry.   It crowns a small wood overlooking an estuary into which countless fleets and ditches drain ; frogs, eels, rats, to say nothing of other trifles that serve to satisfy a heron's appetite, are plentiful.   Few people dwell in that deserted countryside. Farms are of the kind known as " off-hand " and occupied by bailiff, overseer or " looker," as he is variously called, so

HERON

herons should thrive undisturbed, but I have watched nests dwindle from a score until only half a dozen remain. Certainly birds whose homes are in the highest branches of a clump of elms make up in noise for lack of numbers. While mother sits on her bright blue-green eggs, father goes hunting. His flight is stately enough, he makes an attractive picture as he sails homewards, sometimes with an eel in mouth—his bill has serrated edges from which nothing escapes. But, when he leaves the nest, all grace goes ; the first outward movement is awkward, the flier must struggle for balance, while calling all the world to witness that only a big effort could have given him mastery of the air. When there were many nests in tree tops, the immediate vicinity was unpleasant ; these birds drop food from time to time and it decays ; I should not be surprised to learn that even March winds go past a heronry as quickly as they can, and yet the sight of two or three birds on rough platforms of twigs that serve for a nest, with their mates standing like sentinels on branches nearby is not to be forgotten. I saw it once through an hour of an April evening that gilded all trees in turn, an hour, when apart from sunshine and shadow, herons and I seemed to have the world to ourselves. I watched through field glasses from a stile by the road, a road that knew only farmer's wain, carrier's cart and doctor's gig. Now, alas ! char-a-banc and motorbus race up and down, sudden motor cars scatter confusion ; perhaps it is not surprising that herons have gone, no man knows whither.

A very old countryman hobbled down the road and pulled an imaginary forelock. It was Reuben Dunt, known to his fellow when I was young as Ruby, a man who could lay a hedge, clean a ditch, dig a drain or thatch a stack with anybody. Upright then and sturdy, bent now and frail ; recognition was mutual.

" You ain't bin hereabouts same as you useter," he remarked. " I counted you might ha' gone off dead. There's a many bin an' gone since you lived here," and he named men and women we used to know.

" Herons have gone, too," I added, pointing to the distant elms.

" Mos'ly bound to," he explained." They don't like themselves where it's noisy. Caw," he added. " I mind th' time you never heerd nawthen, 'cept it was a farm cart. But there ain't much kin come down my green lane, bein' it don't lead anywheres, an' I kin set in peace. Me married darter lives along o' me now," he went on, " her an' her husban' an' th' child'en."

" Me hearin' ain't what it was," he went on, " but I don't ail anything along o' me eyes, ne yet me fet, an' I got me pension. Caw, when I got married I worked Monday mornin' to Saturday night f'r ten shillin's an' lost some o' that, time th' rine come or the frost. An' now I on'y got to hobble far as th' post office to git it f'r nawthen. That's a rum world," he added, dropping his voice, " though I sez it what shouldn't."

" Which would you prefer," I asked him. " To be young again and able to earn your ten shillings or to be old and get it for nothing ? "

" I'd liefer be as I am," he replied. " That ain't like it used to be. Time me father an' mother was too old to work, they took 'em to th' work-house an' killed 'em quick."

" No," I said, " that's surely wrong, Ruby."

" I lay it ain't," he replied. " They was well enough 'cept they hadn't got enough to eat, an' time they got up there "—he pointed to the far hill, where once the workhouse stood—" they was both dead in three months. Don't tell me. Time th' owd overseer dropped on man or woman, they gotter die."

*   *   *   *

" I don't think nawthen to the herons," the marshland shepherd told me, in days when I had just discovered the heronry, and had been fascinated. He came past the hide in a hedge from which I watched them.

" How is that ? " I asked him.

" When I first got a gun," he explained, pulling at his little clay pipe, " I reckoned I'd get meself a Sunday dinner, so I got up to the grove one mornin' afore it was light an' I set there till I could see, an' time a gre't ole heron came home with a eel in his mouth, I let fly an' knocked him down.

Caw! He took forever o' pluckin', an' he stunk wunnerful, but I kep' on, an' time he wore plucked an' clent there worn't much left o' him. But I cooked him right enough an' tried to eat him, an' got to give him to the cat. Th' on'y thing I got f'r me cartridge was th' eel he wore carryin'. I could eat that. I'd told some o' 'em up at the farm what I done, an' they never let me hear th' last on't. Plaguey things, herons, all said an done.'

36.—BLACK BROOK.

Black Brook, the little stream that passes laughing through the meadows, has abundant occasion for mirth; it sees the best of the gay seasons. A dozen tiny springs renew its strength in the dog days; stately alders rise from the banks, wrens nest in under-growth about their roots, cuckoo calls from high branches, robin did not disdain a hole in the bank for his April home. I have found otters and kept very quiet, for there are butchers about; sportsmen is the name they prefer but don't deserve. Fish swim as happily as though the brook were three times as wide, water vole chooses his ledge and eats daintily. There was one trouble, and that lay in the accumulation of decayed leaves, mud and broken branches where our land ends. If we could clear mud away, shape banks and get down to clean gravel and sand, it would be possible in due season, or so I fondly imagined, to realise my ambition and raise a few trout, keeping them within limits by the aid of fine mesh wire.

So we set to work one bright morning, to find that the block at the boundary end had been made deliberately, perhaps in order to keep ducks or geese from passing over it; stakes had been driven in, oak boards nailed to them, and heavy wire added. It was a long and dirty job to force the prison door and allow the water to pass out with part of the mud in company. Then, with a few iron sheets and some turf at a point a couple of hundred yards further back, we held the water up and the flow ceased. We saw a few small fish and some eels, and were about to start work when our dam collapsed and we had to begin again. We built another, made up of ten-foot iron sheets, an oak door, half

THE BLACK BROOK

a dozen slabs of concrete and a load of boulder clay. It promised to hold enough for a water garden with irises and water lilies, but after a little while broke the promise with a loud report. Clearly it was a job for experts with the right tackle and a proper feeling of what would be due to them for coming in to the wilds to a ditch hardly worth their attention. But before giving in I tried again.

The last effort provided us for a little while with a miniature waterfall, very musical without being too loud, the water flowed sparkling over a bed of sand or gravel. All the dirty clay had been dug out and piled on one side for use on the celery beds. The leaves mixed up in it, sweepings of a dozen autumns, are invaluable and the water would keep bright until autumn overloaded it. When the trees were bare, a few hours' work would set everything to rights ; after all, we had to face the accumulated neglect of many years. I made all these statements and many others equally wise, until the barrier burst again and I told the water quite angrily that it wasn't worth a dam.

Mr. Tripp, to whom I told my story, went so far as to say that in a couple of months, " there won't be a mite o' water 'cept what come out o' th' clouds." Drought was on the land just then, we bandied words.

The Scribe : " Did you ever have a dowser about here ? "

Mr. Tripp (proudly) : " I got a cousin, his father was me own mother's brother. He could take a hazel twig an' show ye water anywheres, leastways (with caution) pervidin' it was there. But there, you ain't got no water over at yours an' never hadn't. You can't tell me you have."

The Scribe (confidently) : " I've found half a dozen springs."

Mr. Tripp : " You dedn't wanter done that ; me cousin could ha' found 'em for ye."

The Scribe (apologetically) : " I hadn't heard of him."

Mr. Tripp (with dignity) : " An' he hadn't heerd o' you, I lay. I count there ain't no water up at yours."

The Scribe : " Why ? "

Mr. Tripp : " If you got water in your part, 'ouldn't I come to hear on't, bein' I've lived in these parts man an' boy, an' got me own pump in me garden what ain't never give out ? A man don't want to send f'r furriners, to look f'r water hereabouts. They don't know nawthen about it. We don't want furriners, ne yet geese from Chiny. Master Studdy bin tellin' me how you bin gooin' on. There ain't no call for sech in these parts. We belong here, they don't. We ain't sheermen."

I remembered that I had given offence by talking in terms of praise about Chinese geese.*

It is an odd fact that in Essex, Suffolk and Norfolk, men from the shires are lumped together as " sheermen," and proclaimed to be of no account. Is this a feeling that dates from the time of the Heptarchy ? It is clear, too, that Mr. Studdy has not forgiven me for keeping Chinese geese, or rather for proposing to keep them.

(* Chapter X.)

CHAPTER VII

SPRING

37.—FROST IN APRIL.

ROUND me are the fruit farmers, no sons of the soil, but
for the most part men with money who have taken to the
work because it is a comparatively new industry in a well-
adapted area. Fruit seems to thrive here when conditions
are good. But three times in as many years the best laid hopes
of those who spare no pains and no outlay in the cultivation
of their land have suffered partial wreck. A fine promising
spring has justified every optimistic estimate and then the
fruit farms have recalled the Master's familiar lines :

> To-day he puts forth
> The tender leaves of hope ; to-morrow blossoms—
> The third day comes a frost, a killing frost
> And—nips the root."

I have a neighbour who is a fruit farmer in the truest sense of the term; he has studied his job and he works on his small holding from early morning to late afternoon doing all that may be done. It is impossible not to admire his industry, even though I believe that modern orcharding which is based upon the free use of poisonous minerals is wrong and must in the long run be harmful to Mother Earth whose reprisals will prove hard to bear. But I went past this neighbour's fields on a Saturday afternoon and he was quite content. His land was clean and in excellent heart, the long rows of Cox's Orange were heavy in bud, the strawberries showed promise of abundant fruit, the cherries were like a shower of snow with the sun on it.

" We're three or four weeks earlier than last year," he said. " Now we have to hope that we shan't have late frosts, or that if they do come, they won't be severe."

The week-end mornings and afternoons were radiant, the nights clear and with an ever deepening cold. On a Sunday night the thermometer registered twelve degrees of frost, Monday morning showed the strawberry plants on my own land bright and shining and the black currant clusters touched with a crimson stain. The apple blossom looked to be un-touched, but if you opened one there was deep discolouration within the stigma.

On the Tuesday I passed my neighbour busy with his cultivator and asked him, a little nervously, how he had fared.

" Like everybody else round here," he replied. " More than half the crop gone." And then, because he is that sort of man, he began to talk of the plight of the big local growers who would be so hard put to find work for their staff and of the village women who earn good money through the summer months picking each crop. I had been told of gales in Worcestershire and frosts in Cambridge, each doing serious damage to blossoming fruit, but trouble afar can never be so real to you as it is in your own and a neighbour's fields. We may have sympathy, but we lack imagination.

Our own fruit has paid a heavy penalty but we grow only for the house and rely in part upon glass. There again we have a south slope with a wood behind it and there is some protection here. Just a few growers can put up a smoke barrage against frost but the cost is said to work out at nearly twenty pounds an acre over a term of years, a notable addition to the costs of production, and the result of burning crude oil that invades neighbouring houses and gardens is so unpleasant that in Kent some growers have been restrained by law ; the Public Health Act of 1936 would appear to offer a much-needed protection.

Apparently late frosts lay an indifferent hand upon England, but I think the grip must needs be heaviest on our East coast. To sense the trouble, think of the work done since the last crop was gathered, the pruning and dressing, the feeding of the soil, ploughing and cleaning, all the preparations to market the crop, the dovetailed arrangements for labour, the rising tide of work, the feverish paces of June, July, and August when the outside help pours in. All this life and activity, all this energy and legitimate aspiration quenched between the dusk of one perfect day and the dawning of another. It looks as though Nature had borrowed her mood from one of the old-time destroyers of humanity or their latter-day reincarnations.

" Ask your wife to come across with you this afternoon when you stop work and we will talk of something else over the tea table for a change," I suggested to my neighbour.

." A good idea," he said. " We'll come." And I asked myself very doubtfully if I could hope to be so brave in like circumstances. The money loss doesn't matter so much, we have all lost our money in our time and not always through our own fault ; it is the uncertainty that strikes us down and forces us to ask *cui bono ?* What profit shall a man have of his labour under the sun ? Perhaps he gets it out of his greater courage to endure, out of his ability to say " My head is bloody but unbowed." I know that when I talked of the trouble to my neighbour over beyond the wood I was talking to a plucky man.

On the farm, troubles come gradually if at all. Should the rain spoil the hay it will swell the roots, should drought parch the roots, the sun will ripen the corn. If pig prices are down, sheep may be a good market, there is always time for recovery and readjustment, or so it seemed to me when I was farming. But where trouble comes like a bolt from the blue, rapid as an epileptic stroke, or a motor-car accident, only courage, and a fine courage at that, avails. One can but hope that when our own testing time comes we may remember and emulate.

38.—" THE PEACE OF THE WOODS."

If there be a time of year when the appeal of wood and wold is specially compelling, it is the month of May. All migrants are in full song, the last visitors, swift, spotted fly-catcher and night-jar have arrived. Thrushes are nesting for a second time, corncrake is heard on the arable where his nest is in making, the last of winter visitors has long gone home. The wood carries a carpet of bluebells, a few purple and spotted orchids are rising, ferns unfolding, the wild cherry is in flower, so too are holly trees. Insect life is abroad, round blossoming crab-apples bee music may be heard all day ; the clustered white flowers of the guelder rose shine in the sun. The wood is very still, bird song and hum of insect almost the only sounds, no intruders break upon the solitude for holiday season has not come round ; it is too late for poachers to search for pheasant's eggs, children are at school, labour is busy on the land. Talk casually of woodland in Maytime to the man whose life chains him to a great city, and you may feel suddenly ashamed. Such speech sounds like a boast.

Where the wood falls away along a hillside, in a corner from which one can overlook the best of the flowering trees, I sat with a town friend who said suddenly : " What a haunt of unbroken peace."

I replied : " You are wrong ; it is a scene of unending war," and a moment later the harsh cries of a couple of quarrelsome jays sounded close by. They came to the near branch of a beech tree, saw us and made off, the sun gilding the bright blue feathers on their wings as they disappeared.

It is all too easy to talk of sanctuary, of reserves where bird and beast shall be free from persecution, but the ideal is not attainable. To give harmless life its chance you must repress its enemies.

The other morning I passed a stoat. She did not glare for a moment and run away after the fashion of stoats, with eyes that reveal the most startling colour in the sunlight; she stood still, arched her back and hissed, telling me that she had young nearby and was prepared to defend them to the death. It would have been cruel to kill her in that hour, but it was not easy to turn away and leave her undisturbed for she will range the wood and kill baby rabbits and birds in order not only to feed her young but to gratify her blood lust. Perhaps she will solve the problem that was too hard for me by running through one of the box traps set here and there in the wood. Now and again you may see a hedgehog walking cautiously along and because he will take some of the eggs from birds that nest on the ground, gamekeepers kill on sight. But I think he deserves protection and act accordingly. Why spare hedgehog and persecute rat, stoat and weasel? This isn't an easy question to answer; I meet it by pointing out that the three last named can get away easily, while hedgehog's movements are slow, and for half the year he sleeps.

What about jay, magpie, hawk? They are cruel and merciless, no harmless bird is safe from their attack. Eggs, fledglings, even adult birds, if their enemy can get at them, are destroyed. Yet sparrowhawk and kestrel are beautiful, their flight a joy to the eye, while jay and magpie lend vivid colour to the woodland scene. How can one deal with these birds that live on others? I don't know the best way, but I have my own. I tell the gardener to walk through the woods when the nests are built and the eggs are laid and if they cannot be reached by safe climbing, to put a charge of shot through them. In this fashion the living are spared and sometimes, when their homes are destroyed, raptorial birds leave the neighbourhood. Sparrows' nests are removed, too, but so soon as one nest is taken they start to build another. It sounds cold-blooded but when you have suffered a real invasion of sparrows you will be anxious to keep them within limits and, so far as other birds are concerned, you have but to go through garden or wood and see nests that blackbird, thrush and hedge-sparrow have deserted because bigger and stronger birds have robbed them of eggs or fledglings. We owe all three something for their song, the thrush perhaps most of all, because he sings when boughs are bare.

Another robber to be suppressed is the jackdaw, and the job is not easy, because he nests so wisely. Those near me have chosen to build in trees or, to be precise, in holes where the wood is rotting. They do not make a nest hole like the woodpeckers, but select one that nature has made and when the young are hatched they hunt in couples. Amusing birds and intelligent pets, but if you want to protect songsters you can't preserve jackdaws. Magpies build domed nests very often out of reach and hard to damage, the jay does not give so much trouble. His nest is readily found; his harsh cry when on the warpath is a warning, although but a useless one, to small birds. They may be able to get away but they can't save eggs or nestlings, and from the day when thrush and blackbird lead the van and build their nests in bushes that new born spring has found no time to cover, down to the season when the partridge has hatched her clutch and the passionate symphony of song is fading from the woods, this slaughter of innocents goes on. It is not surprising to hear that experts place the number of casualties in bird land at something like seventy-five per cent; it is more surprising that there should be twenty-five per cent of survivors. The season of greatest loss is, I believe, early morning when flesh-eating birds are out for their breakfast and the rest of the world is asleep. I have noticed nests that have carried a full clutch in the late afternoon have been empty at eight o'clock on the following day.

What is the reaction in birdland ?　We all know that a tiny finch will fight for her young ; that the mother rabbit will even defend her babies against the stoat ; that the wren will attack the weasel.　But for how long do they sense loss ? In early morning, following the beginning of April, I often lie awake and listen to the first chorus, one that opens and dies down as though it were just a prelude, a hymn to the rising sun.　It never varies or diminishes though, as soon as the songs are sung and the birds are foraging for their young, all the merciless army of free-booters will be at work round me. You know the hour when the first few uncertain notes are sounded " the opening pipe of half-awakened birds," the full outburst and then silence.　In that stillness, eggs are being stolen, young birds torn to pieces, grim death is passing along hedgerow, penetrating the woodland fastness.　There is no outcry from the wood, unless stoat or weasel is in pursuit of rabbit.　I keep no steel traps here for rabbits to be broken in, snares are of the humane kind, but you will not stop a hungry fox or poacher cat from pouncing on a rabbit that can't get away.

Congratulate yourself on running a woodland sanctuary if you will, on opening a winter hostel for birds, on protecting squirrels, grass snakes, hedgehogs and other hunted creatures, but the best you can do is woefully incomplete.　There are gaps in the shelter you have built, gaps through which death can slip at any hour of day or night.　Only one cause for mild satisfaction remains—if you did not help, conditions would be worse.　You do know of certain birds that have been enabled to bring their young to maturity, of enemies that can't multiply their species for another year at least. Are we justified in our efforts ?　Can you say ?　I only know that I dare not talk of " the peace of the woods."　I must leave this to my confident friends.

39.—A Shepherd.

You can walk for miles through the smiling Suffolk valley and see no more than scattered farmhouses.　Pleasant and pastoral, this corner of the country maintains a limited number of farmers and their workers in content if not in comfort.

THE SHEPHERD

They are the heirs to a tradition, they are doing as their fathers
and grandsires have done for many generations. It is the
country of black-faced sheep. Time was when they made
fortunes, built churches and founded families, such was the
power of wool. To-day, they have no such gift, though the
pastures are still sound and there is sufficient water, lower in a
very dry season; if rail and motor bus stay afar, nobody
worries over much. Progress may never come back to
this corner of the world, even for a holiday.

We left the valley for the hillside, a mild ascent that led
to a great field of temporary pasture, grasses sown for one, two,
or even three years' service. This one was not so rich as it
might and should have been just then, the drought of yester-
year had weighed too heavily upon it, but there was enough
for a flock of the short-wool Suffolk-down sheep, the ones
whose faces look as though they had been oiled and brushed.
They were with their lambs all enjoying the sunlight, as happy
as animals can be. A shrivelled old man was in charge.

" Sixty year ago, I started to help me father," he told me, " an' I've had charge o' th' flock most fifty."

" A pleasant life in fine weather," I said, " and when lambing is over."

" Aye," he replied, " I'm always glad when the yowes (ewes) are through their troubles. There's some of them won't have 'em any more, they'll be cast an' fatted." Somehow this did not seem to be in the right key ; I could but feel sorry for the silly sheep, and said so.

The shepherd reproved me.

" They've had their time an' bin well cared f'r," he reminded me. " The lambs won't do so well. They won't have as much as a summer. I'll be pickin' out tharty to-morrow to go to market."

" Will you miss them ? " I asked him.

" Sheep come an' go," he answered, " an' we do the same. Master is th' gran'son of the man I started with, so you see th' butcher don't make such a lot o' difference. An' mark you," he added, as the light came to him, " if nobody wanted lamb or mutton nobody 'd keep sheep. Folk don't want to take trouble for nothin'."

CHAPTER VIII

FRIENDS ON THE WING

40.—DAWN.

In town, factory hooters proclaim the dawn, here bird song anticipates it. With the aid of a pair of glasses, it is possible to watch wild life soon after it is astir in wood and garden. The early morning light floods the elm trunks with gold, revealing sundry finches searching for breakfast, giving the woodpecker a very shining red helmet, a very fine green cloak. He greets the dawn with a noisy laugh and then passes in waving flight over the house to the wood where you can sometimes hear him hammering on the bark of trees that have seen their best days. Soon every bird calls to the sun.

We have our share of the night cries, though nightingales are never too clamorous here in the brief season of their song. But there are at least three owls, the white Barn Owl that hisses as he flies, the Brown Owl that calls sadly from the wood, and the Little Owl that has brought the family into disrepute, but has at long last received a certificate of harmlessness to the great annoyance of some gamekeepers.

Blackbirds call during the night when the cuckoo disturbs them, you hear rabbits scream, sometimes fox and vixen exchange a call across the valley. These are the common cries and in the dawn hours there comes a brief spell in which every singing bird proclaims that it is well awake—and then sallies forth in pursuit of that unfortunate early worm. Why do early birds win praise while the still earlier effort of the worm is ignored?

Neither bird nor worm is always first afield. A recent morning broke so pleasantly that the temptation to rise a few minutes later was irresistible. Dew was on the grass, goloshes were clearly indicated, and I walked softly through the wood to see if any interesting wild life was astir by Black Brook. It was a little before six o'clock by Summer Time, and the land was hardly awake.

I saw no birds and no farm workers were afield, but I saw in the next meadow a gentleman who carried a sack over his shoulder. He walked delicately but swiftly to a point by the wood's edge, picked up a snare and put it in his pocket, then to another corner where he picked up something, presumably a rabbit. His morning business was now over, he stepped across the meadow and climbed over the gate with commendable agility. I did not see his face, but his build was not altogether unfamiliar. Is it possible that he is one of the philanthropists who has offered to catch my rabbits? I can only presume that my neighbours have taken advantage of a similar offer and given him the wrong direction as to boundaries. No other explanation is possible for I remember quite distinctly that he told me he was a right-forward man. Unfortunately I have left in the wallet on Time's back the years in which I could have caught him up and asked him to set my doubts at rest. Now, if a man has a one field start of me, he can get away with anything. I can only catch him by telephone.

41.—THE ORDER OF SONG.

To-day, even if you wake before sunrise, anywhere outside the circle of great cities and manufacturing towns, you can hear a full bird chorus, so full indeed that only an expert can identify the varied notes. When, as here, the bedroom is shadowed by a wood and you have windows on three sides, the faint, uncertain cries in which some singers ask the darkness if daybreak is near at hand, come faintly through, and by one window I can watch the answer glowing in the east. In despair of dividing up the chorus I have turned back to my notes to see how it started.

In January the only bold singer was the missel thrush; he would sit on the top of larch or ash tree and assure some unseen lady-love that winter could not endure.

In the early afternoon of fine days, I heard his cousin, the song thrush, singing softly, as an opera singer does at rehearsal when he wishes to save his voice. The little tree creeper that favours an oak by the summerhouse would be vocal now and again; so would the robin and, more rarely, the wren. It was not until January was nearly out that, just before sunset, a blackbird burst into song on an elm branch. The tits sounded a few faint notes as they came to and from the pieces of fat suspended from branches on pieces of string; very gladly we had disfigured the garden for their sakes. In the wood jays screamed and brown owls hooted through the darkness, but one cannot add their notes to song.

My diary tells me that the earliest full evening chorus of birds was heard in the opening week of February and the first morning chorus two days later. Missel and song thrush, blackbird, hedge sparrow, longtailed tit and chaffinch took part and there were some other notes that I could not be sure about. As I write it seems impossible that the world should have lacked bird song or that it should have been difficult to recognise the few singers; from quartet or quintet to full orchestra is such a far cry.

I returned here one Spring from the south country of the Alpes Maritimes where it had been a rare event to hear a bird sing. It was more than their lives were worth to warn "sportsmen" that they were about. There is a close season but there is no authority to enforce its observance. In every town you could buy thrushes, larks, and blackbirds, even the tiny finch was not despised.

The explanation was given to me by the intelligent mayor of a small Provençal town.

"We haven't two thousand people here," he told me, "and there are between two and three hundred gun licences taken out at fifty francs. Think what all this licence money must come to when half the men of any village go out with their guns. The Government can't afford to lose the revenue."

42.—BIRD-NESTING WITH A PERISCOPE.

The wild cherry trees were covered with a white veil of blossoms in whose folds bees, past numbering, made music ; larches wore their tenderest green, blackthorn looked as though the last of winter's snow had lingered on bare branches. Silver birch was in leaf, elm and oak, beech and alder were moving more slowly towards green hours, but the urge of the horse chestnut could no longer be restrained and all its buds were breaking. Even privet and rhododendron, elder and honeysuckle had thrust forward new leaves, meadowland had been patterned by the harrow. The wood was waiting expectantly, hopefully, looking for a warm south wind with, for choice, a shower or two in its train.

Because April had been so shy, it was early to go nest hunting, but there would be some reward apart from the joy of a Spring time ramble in the wood. Bluebells were giving the earliest flush of colour to the ground, foxglove was spreading broad leaves, mauve cuckoo-flower clustered under the hedges, everywhere birds cried the joys of the season. "For lo," they sang, " the spring is here, the winter is over and gone, the time of our singing has come."

As though to emphasise the seclusion of woodland the first distinctive cry to be heard above the song of finches and warblers was a curious trilling note that might recall the nightjar. Then from ash to beech tree the great spotted woodpecker, a vision of bright feathers, black, scarlet and white, flashed across and was lost. He is not great if compared with the green woodpecker, whose challenging cry can be heard afar, perhaps he is three or four inches shorter ; he has a black bill while his green cousin has a grey one.

Doubtless he was watching the intruders from some tall stem round which he would peep cautiously, but he must have gone awing again speedily, for his cry grew faint. The home he was building stood revealed about fifteen feet above the ground in an ash tree that had seen the last of its useful days, the hole had been made quite recently, the bark was freshly chiselled. You could hear his cry now. It was like drum taps, but the " French Magpie," as old countrymen call him, was not hammering for a home ; he was signalling to his mate. Curiously enough the new hole is no more than a yard above an old one worn smooth by use and rains. In all probability the lower nest has been taken by starlings, they enjoy the thrill of ousting a woodpecker and are busy with their families before the rarer bird has found his wife again.

We stopped awhile under the flowering cherry tree to watch a cuckoo taking hawklike flight across the valleys, calling as he flew, and then dipped down to the wood's verge where the garden warbler, the one migrant that can challenge the nightingale, was singing lustily, almost carelessly. He permitted us to come within a few yards of the branch from which he scattered music to the Spring morning. How the little olive brown bird can spread so much sweetness is past understanding and the pæan is sounded for joy of life ; nesting season must wait until the cover is thick enough to hide the nest with its moss and horsehair and half-dozen eggs, speckled on a white ground. He is not like the thrush and blackbird whose ill-protected homes, some already rifled by magpies or jays, stare at us from bare branches. A nightingale was in full midday song across the valley, it would be hard to choose between him and his rival, each song is full of the spirit of the opening year.

While we waited to listen to the fresh music, a little tree creeper ran up an elm trunk looking for insects, and then flew down again to resume his rapid search with really remarkable industry. As he passed from tree to tree it was possible to see him resting on his tail while his quick thin beak was working. Somewhere under the yielding bark of an old tree he will build a nest, perhaps the nest is already in the making. We had but to rest awhile and baby rabbits appeared on all sides looking with innocent surprise at the strangers. The vixen had left the wood taking her cubs with her, half a dozen stoats had been shot, a reign of terror had ended.

Two rare birds not to be mistaken for any others flew across a corner of the meadow on their way to some Douglas firs where their nest is built well out on a branch. They were cross-bills, the male's dress touched with scarlet, the female's with greenish yellow. They are here because the conifers yield cones with seeds that they prefer to insects and small fruit of the later months. Year after year they come back but are very shy and would not have been seen had we not been standing still to admire the nest of a wren, built into the ivy that has gathered round and strangled a hedgerow elm.

Behind the holly bush nightingale was singing loudly. Building was just about to begin. There will be six weeks more of full song and then the glory will depart and the music of the world's most famous songster become a mere harsh croak. Several nightingales live here and, because they are undisturbed, return. What are their land or sea marks? Are they the parents or the children of the May that passed a year ago? Nobody knows or, at least, nobody tells us.

In the fork of an elder bush chaffinches have built. The mother slipped off at our approach but only for a few yards and then as the periscope was pushed gently through the branches to show the progress of nesting she became excited and fluttered round within a few inches of the glass which revealed three eggs. So soon as it was withdrawn she flew back to look out with frightened eyes and perhaps rejoice in our departure. In a few days the growth of greenery will hide her completely. At present she must needs fear the magpie and the jay. By the way, a small mirror at the end of a collapsible fishing rod makes a simple and effective periscope. You can see many nests without climbing and without frightening the owners.

Robin, thrush and blackbird, their eggs ill-protected against prying and unfriendly eyes, had contrived to rear first broods, there were a few young thrushes hopping about awkwardly with guardian parents anxious in the background. February, March and April seem alike to this sweetest of singers; three broods, if not four, are needed to make up for the slaughter of the innocents. Robin, like thrush, builds in February or

March, but is not so prolific and to-day the killing of robins, once a popular pastime, is nowhere encouraged.   One tin can that served for a home last year had not been favoured ; perhaps we looked at it too often, but robin, ever friendly, followed us from bush to bush as though feeling we should be the happier if we had his company as well as his song.

A jay swept across a clearing, sounding a note that is doubly unpleasant, first because it reminded us that he is a marauder, and secondly, because we knew that if we could find his nest before the young are hatched we should have no choice but to destroy it that harmless birds may have their homes, eggs, and, in many cases, fledglings " when April melts in Maytime." As things happened we had a full morning's bird-nesting, seeing without touching, and no bird was the worse for our ramble.

43.—YAFFLE.

On an ash tree a green woodpecker, very gay in his summer dress, brought a long, undulating flight to a close.   A moment later a magpie lit on an upper branch and uttered his harsh cry.   " Yaffle," as the woodpecker is called, responded at once with a louder call which was answered quickly from the wood as his wife left her station, perhaps her nest, to join him.   I waited, expecting that there would be trouble, begun, of course, by the magpie, but either he does not attack woodpeckers or he is afraid to attack a pair, for nothing happened. Had he tried to interfere, they would probably have run round the tree-trunk and dodged him, until he had to fly away baffled and beaten.

44.—CONTEMPT.

There is a warm, secluded corner where our woodland meets that of a neighbour.   A summerhouse is set amidst brambles that call for trimming and there are unsightly rushes that can only be killed by the aid of a drain that will carry off the water on which they thrive.   Yet it is a snug retreat ; when I settle in with books and papers, word passes that I have gone for a walk without saying when I shall return.

To sit in the summerhouse day by day and win the disregard of those who live there is to grasp the measure of your own insignificance, to become conscious of a little kingdom that holds you in no regard. At first there might have been some unease, but wild life has learned that there is nothing to be fearful about and is content. Young birds fly under the eyes of parents, wood pigeons burdened by domestic occasions criticise them across fir-tree tops. A noisy jay occasions more concern than I do.

All round me the life of wood and hedgerow ignores the intruder. I can hear the migrants sing to their nesting mates, the patter of a scurrying rabbit, perhaps a descendant of the one Alice met in Wonderland, hurrying across last year's dried leaves on the floor of the wood. If the wind be right, it carries garden perfume on invisible pinions ; I can hear the hushed note of Black Brook " which to the quiet woods all night, singeth a quiet tune."

Stray foraging bees come to the bowl of early flowers on my table and sip, and robin waits long enough to see if I have any stock of crumbs. Red squirrel looks down from the branches of a chestnut tree, not, I am sure, without contempt for the awkward human who cannot run up a perpendicular trunk, to whom a jump from one bough to another across a space two or three times his own length would never have been possible. A few days ago a young rabbit squeezed through small mesh wire that should guard the garden round my work-shop and fed shamelessly. If the lurcher had not seen her she would have stayed until she had grown too big to escape. As things happened she carried away a whole skin, first round one tree and then round another in fashion that disgusted her pursuer.

I have been the only watcher of the pageant of seasons in this space of woodland from the time when daffodils shed their light across the enclosure and narcissi followed with bluebells and lupins and a few stray lilies of the valley. I have watched gorse blaze and die, broom come to flower, beech and chestnut clothe their nakedness until their vesture could hide the sun ; while on the bared floors of the wood to which light came less than a year ago elder and bramble begin to stake new claims. All life around me, beast or bird, tree, bush or flower is curiously detached and aloof. I have no part therein,

THE SUMMERHOUSE

though I watch with keenest eyes as it passes in procession from birth to death.

The two turtle doves that have come over here to spend a quiet Spring and Summer, ignored strangers. Their nest overlooks the summerhouse, my presence gives them no concern; they walked on the grass patch in front, the small space of greenery that rabbits cannot invade. They looked at me and at the lurcher by my side and went on with their conversation. Even wood pigeon in the spruce fir continued to utter her pleasantly monotonous note and when she flew away with a great clatter of wings it was on account of a couple of red squirrels. They haunt the wood, partly because it holds hazel bushes and Spanish chestnut trees and partly because the gardener takes house scraps to the chickens. I did not know how fond squirrels are of little pieces of fat for a *bonne bouche* until I watched them race down tree trunks, snatch their prize and run away. Whether they ate or hid the spoils just then it is hard to say because I couldn't see and could not leave my work.

Through the window behind me came a sudden burst of

song from a gold crest ; it might have gone unidentified but for the nest under the overhanging branch of a larch.   I can only catch the pleasant notes if the wind is favourable. Indeed, when all the migrants have come to swell the early summer choir it is very difficult to recognise songs with any approach to certainty, particularly if you are busy with books.   I remember watching the gold crests at work on a nest in the Spring of last year.   Nothing could have been better balanced or more delicate ; they had chosen a plum tree instead of a conifer, though conifers were all round, but when the work was complete they disappeared and the home stood deserted, another example of what old country folk call " cocks' nests."

A magnificent queen hornet has flown into the summer-house and I had to ask myself very seriously if she should live or die.   Nature must have a place for hornets in her scheme of things, even though we ignore the obvious truth, but there are too many old and rotten trees in the neglected woods round here, and if hornets have another favouring summer we may find trouble.   On the other hand, when you are enjoying sunshine and summer days, have you the right to destroy lower forms of the one life that stretches from mineral to human, and perhaps below and above these limits in realms we cannot conceive ?   " You not only disturb me," I said to the hornet reproachfully, " but you present me with a difficult problem."   Thereupon the lady resolved my doubts and difficulties by flying out of the summerhouse and up into the sunshine ; I thanked her much for that.

The tumbler pigeons have been practising exhibition flights, high above the wood, with a certain show sense that would do credit to a circus manager.   At first they go round in a wide circle and then proceed to perform their tricks, falling through the air as though their wings had failed them, recovering when and where they please, turning back somersaults.   I think airmen who give exhibitions of trick flying have something to learn from tumbler pigeons ; certainly the latter never crash.   I watch with a certain apprehension because, should they see me, they will come round to demand dari, and as I have none in my pocket, this will mean a return to the house, and when you are busy——

A cloud has veiled the sun. What a difference it makes !
The tree tops bow to a harsh gust, from an elder bush a blackbird scolds heartily. His remonstrance is not without effect ;
the sun breaks through again and the wind dies down.

45.—WORK AND PLAY.

It may be supposed that robins work as hard as other
birds, but they don't realise that men also have their jobs.
Just as I am about to make a note, the robin with whom I am
on good terms, flies down to a branch of the stunted beech,
puts his head on one side and asks with eye rather than
tongue—" What have you for me ? " He looks sleek and
well fed, has forgotten all about the winter and has helped to
raise a family in a tin can not twenty yards away. He does
not know that it was set there to tempt some bird to accept
a rainproof nest, but such security as it gave his wife, self and
family may account for the sleek, well-groomed appearance.
" It is impossible to read books and feed robins, more than
ever impossible when your pockets are empty." These
words, spoken harshly, cause him to fly away, a little surprised, for as a rule I make much of him.

A company of goldfinches is at play among the larches.
There are half a dozen, parents and family perhaps, the glass
will tell. Yes, there are two adults and four youngsters, and
they fly away suddenly to a great clump of cornflowers. The
flowers are out of sight but they go in their direction, where
I have seen them for some days past. The parents must have
built near by, so did the whitethroats. The nettle clump
hid their nest and was allowed to stand for their sakes until
the young were fledged. There are times when father white-
throat responds with snatches of song ; the payment is quite
satisfactory.

Now I am waiting for something to happen. Sun is
shining, but birds are silent, a stray butterfly flits across unchallenged, insects should be humming as they play in the
warm air, but there is no sound. Even breezes are still.
It is a sleepy hour. Who will break the summer silence ?
Robin or blackbird, long-tailed tit perhaps, one flew past
a moment ago. If I were a gambler I would lay myself a
great wager that it will be the tit ; the money would be lost.

First comes a distant cock crow, then a dog barks, and after that comes a song by a modest hedge sparrow. And the next sound ? Perhaps the jay that dived through the tangle of firs. But no, it is the very different call of the lunch bell.

46.—MORNING.

Pigeon parliament assembles on the gable ridge shortly after daylight at this season. The members look infinitely wise, say very little and sit with stark ruffled feathers if there should be any suspicion of chill in the air. After a time they walk along the ridge to look for water and if, as often happens, I am in the bathroom by that hour, I throw some out that it can run on to the gutter. Although they are all very thirsty and will not venture as far as Black Brook at a time when hawks are about, they retreat in alarm so soon as I supply their needs. When the window is closed and I am invisible, they return to the ridge and a little later the boldest sidles to the water and drinks. After that, you can't see the gutter for feathers.

In the meantime, from an ash tree top a sparrow hawk takes his observation post to look at cottage and pigeons for quite a long time, letting " I dare not " wait upon " I would." On the rim of the wood several birds are in charge of young families that will very presently go out into the world, a hen pheasant brings quite a large following to drink at the stream, sometimes a poaching dog, trying to appear quite innocent, trots gaily along the woodside on his way to the village. Across the valley two cocks express the contempt each holds for the other. A heron often flies high above Black Brook but is not tempted to stay. Not far away, a reaping machine may be at work, the sound is musical in this place and at this hour, and when Summer and Autumn meet they make melody that is not yet written in the minor key.

47.—BEES.

I went to see an old friend, a shoemaker, who is also a beekeeper, and found him sitting among his hives instead of at his bench. It was a Sunday afternoon.

" You're quite safe," he said, making room for me on the garden seat. " There isn't an ounce of trouble in them this afternoon, they're too busy. They want pollen for the young brood, and the re's a bit of blossom honey about. If you were a smoker or a drinker," he added with a smile, " that'd be different. I had Master Cant here last Sunday and I told him to keep at the far end of the garden."

" What happened ? " I asked.

" He said," continued Mr. Bunting, " that he didn't care about a lot of plaguey bees. I think he'd had an extra glass with his dinner. He was glad to run away with only one sting before he got to where you're sitting. Didn't like it because I told him he'd murdered a bee."

" Do you read the papers, Tim ? " I asked him.

" No," he answered. " I take one in the winter when I've shut the hives up, but drop it come April when the bees are getting about. I have my wireless and that gives me a band o' music come the evening. I don't like to listen to folk talking. I get all the talking I want in me shop."

He stopped to point out the colours of the pollen that the bees were bringing home, each bee having bags of one colour, though in the cells all the pollens would be mixed indiscriminately.

" We're lucky here," he went on. " None of your big orchards with poisons sprayed on them and bees being killed off when they go to the blossoms. If there ever was a wrong thing in this world, that's it. If folk like a dash o' poison in their fruit, let 'em have it, but why should the bees that work for us suffer ? Thank the Lord all the fruit round here is in gardens and the blossoms are wholesome. There ought to be a law to protect bees."

" There are all manner of laws needed to protect humans," I remarked, thinking of news that old Timothy Bunting would never hear about.

" People are sensible enough to look after themselves," he persisted, " or they ought to be, but bees look to us to do the right thing by 'em. If everybody in the world had enough honey, there wouldn't be much work for the doctors ne yet the chemists. I've been keeping bees these fifty years or more, so I reckon I know. I'd like to see people making beehives instead of all these armaments we hear tell about. They'd be a sight more useful. I'd liefer have a extry hive than the biggest gun they got in the army."

CHAPTER IX

MORE COUNTRY FOLK

48.—Philosophy in a Garden.

" There ain't a much in it," said Miss Betts. She had come up to the garden gate of her cottage at a moment when I had paused to divide my admiration between a Daphne bush in bloom and the proud legend " Tea's "—the apostrophe is in common use round here, giving an air of refinement to an otherwise bald announcement. " Do you mean garden or business ? " I enquired.

" Each of the both of 'em," replied the proprietress, for she was no less. " If I get a dozen teas over the week-end this time o' year, I think meself lucky. And as for the garden, I've lost the winter flowers and the spring ones aren't really worth while yet."

" You see," explained Miss Betts, " you don't want more than a handful of Christmas roses an' snowdrops an' aconite to make a show with. You're grateful for anything just then, the garden's so bare. Crocuses don't get a chance here ; sparrows are too mischie'ful.

" As for daffodils an' narciss," continued Miss Betts a little resentfully, " it's all or nothin'. You must be smuddered up or nobody thinks you're anything. The same with tulips an' hyacinths, and they're a bit too showy for my taste anyway. There's no betwixt an' between."

" You see," said Miss Betts later, when I had taken a cup of really hot tea, " folk are same as aconite an' snowdrops just now. I set a store by you because you're not a many. Come the summer I'll be tired o' servin' tea an' cuttin' dead roses an' cleaning flower beds. Now a few teas an' a few flowers are everything I look for. It isn't so much what you get in this world as what you think of it when it comes."

" You're a philosopher," I said.

" I don't know about that," replied Miss Betts, " but when you've lived by yourself ten months out of twelve these fifteen year, you do know what you think about things."

" Ten months out of twelve ? " I repeated.

" I got relations," explained Miss Betts sarcastically, " an' they just love the country—any time between middle o' July an' middle o' September. They like to go out and take their lunch with them an' come back late-ish to tea an' something hot with it. You've only one pair o' hands, but, Lord love you, they don't trouble about that, even if you have took them in for next to nothing."

" Folk nowadays," Miss Betts remarked darkly, " want you to work y'r fingers to th' bone an' I'm not going to do it at my time of life, t'ain't likely." She is middle-aged and swarthy, her voice is deep, masculine and minatory.

I waited patiently, convinced that very presently she would ease her bosom of much perilous stuff.

" When I started in business," continued Miss Betts, " the baker was good enough for people and so was the grocer. That was afore the last war. Nowadays," she continued angrily, glad of an audience, " folk put upon you, leastways they try to, but Martha Betts is one too much for 'em. She on't be trod on."

" All last summer," cried the lady, " I got nothing but grumbling. Why dedn't I peck fresh fruit? Why wasn't the water boiling? Couldn't they have an extry jug o' milk, time I hadn't a drain left? "

" I told 'em the baker wouldn't call but twice a week, if anybody went on their bended knees to him, an' that th' dairy farm's half a mile away, an' that I bought th' shop's best jam and that if I pecked fruit and they dedn't come, that wouldn't keep and they wouldn't pay for it. I told 'em fires will go down whiles, an' that I can't be in two places at once. But nothin' satisfied 'em, they kep' on grumblin', an' now they got to go without and serve them right."

I don't think they will go without; they will merely go elsewhere. Miss Betts will be the sole mourner at her custom's funeral, but I did not tell her so. I merely said, with due solemnity, that there is no accounting in this world for the ways of some people, that the more you do the more you may, and that a worm will turn. Then I followed the worm's example, but if I am not mistaken the lady of tea's was not so dissatisfied with me as she had been with her other customers.

49.—SIMPLE COUNTRY MEN.

Poultry houses have passed from the hillside but not so rapidly as I could wish—the last outstayed its welcome by four years. I then sold it for a third of what it must have cost to put up and rejoiced in my good fortune. In the first days of our sojourn I engaged an aged man to lime them within and tar them without, that they might be better fit for disposal; he accepted standard wages, plus overtime. Naturally of thoughtful disposition, his outlook was wide. He had noticed the presence of rabbits on what was to be garden ground, he gave some of his overtime to setting "yokes," a task to which he brought a certain skill and a long experience, but, I hasten to add, charged me nothing for taking away the catch in decent, unobtrusive fashion. The "tradesmen" found in his activities a pleasant foil to their own; they gave a lot of leisure to kindly observation and bought rabbits at less than market price current.

The elderly man had an idea that fowl houses do not like too much lime in one application, so he put on a thin coat sparingly, in preparation, he told me blandly, for another later on. He had two pails for tar in the valley and there was a barrel on the hill top; he would stand by the empty pail for more than half an hour while it changed status and became a full one; tar runs very slowly in cold weather. Then he would take it down to a little fire and stand by while it "hotted up." An engaging old gentleman, he seemed to be a part of the picture in the first few weeks, when our visits to the cottage were made at intervals for a few hours at a time. Then came a morning when I watched him spend just three-quarters of an hour in contemplation, and decided that life would be less costly without him. So far as I could tell the work on the houses would be so prolonged that by the time the last one was left unfinished the first one would need further attention. As he was aging it was clear that he would never catch up with the job. So I told him kindly, gently and gratefully that much though I must regret the parting the time had come to detach him from the houses he had served so long. He went away content; I think my patience had exceeded his most sanguine hopes—and if I was correctly informed later on he had trapped quite a fair number of rabbits.

" Nasty little mucks," he described them to me once, rather ungratefully I thought.

We wanted to set one of the fowl houses in the corner out of sight but in use, and I examined the largest ; fifty feet long and well built, it was equipped with nest boxes and other gadgets. Looking to the sun and with wired run round both sides, it should give birds all the light of a fine day with a little shade on the north where the run stretches to the wood. The light was strong as I went carefully through the house and saw that the perch ends and boxes were infested with red mite ; their movement on the wood faintly perceptible. When the outside was tarred and the inside limewashed by my aged friend, he left the boxes out, though I've no doubt but that he would have come to them in a later year. There had been no birds in that house for several seasons, but red mite had persisted. How had they managed to thrive without their hosts ? A blow lamp is the cure for them, followed by the application of paraffin to all points at which perches touch the sides of walls on the central partition. As the house stood there was sufficient insect life to make poultry keeping a failure. Before the inside was treated, the sides were creosoted and this work revealed one or two defective boards through which rats had travelled to and fro.

That empty house told the full story of old-time careless-ness, explained perhaps the financial collapse that left the cottage standing lonely on the hillside and gave the land to waste. Red mite, rats, laziness and profitable poultry farming never yet went together, but you may find them trying to do so if you look round carefully. The two unsuccessful poultry keepers are the man who neglects his job and the man who tries to exploit his birds and forgets that Nature can only be conquered by obedience.

50.—A TRAMP.

I have found an interesting tramp, a man who takes his life seriously. He passed us as we were packing the remains of a roadside lunch ; without undue pressure he sat down by the road and ate it with appreciation. A grizzled wanderer with tanned skin and laughing eyes, he was poorly clad but

THE TRAMP

decently shod ; he carried a stout ash stick and a considerable shoulder pack that he seemed glad to lay aside. We chatted.

The Tramp : " I go into the House, come the winter. It's warm and they don't treat you too bad in some of 'em now-adays, when you go in for keeps. In the Spring round about Easter I take to the road—you people help a bit."

The Scribe : " With food ? "

The Tramp (nodding) : " When I see a really pretty spot for stopping at, I hang about. More often than not somebody comes to eat and drink. I see 'em and they don't see me. But when they're packing up I come along and pass 'em the time o' day, as I did to you a few minutes ago. If folks are feeling comfortable inside they remember you got a stummick, too. Sometimes I've had enough given me for supper."

The Scribe : " Where do you sleep ? "

The Tramp : " Shed or barn, or under a hedge. Some farmers are all right, if you tell 'em you don't smoke and don't carry matches. You must hide them, an' keep 'em hidden."

The Scribe : " What about rats ? "

The Tramp : " They don't seem to worry a man. I've had 'em run over me, but they've never done me no hurt."

The Scribe : " Do you get jobs ? "

The Tramp : " Bit of hay making, pea picking, fruit picking, helping at fairs. I got my boots out of a hay-making job. Your feet are more than your stomach when you're on the road. If your boots go too far, they get past mending and you're in trouble."

The Scribe : " Who are the most helpful ? "

The Tramp (pausing to light a short clay pipe and think) : " Talking 'em all round, poor folk and the old 'uns at that. Picnic parties give you the best vittles, but they can spare 'em. Only last week a widow woman living by the road saw me pass and asked if I'd like a cup of tea. I'd been washing my second pair of socks and she darned one of them for me, and gave me this stick ; said it belonged to her husband, and it might help me on the road. She's got a daughter in service who pays her rent, half-a-crown a week, and she's got an old age pension. That's all. I'd a few shillings on me for once in a way, just finished a job, and I wanted her to take one. She wouldn't look at it ; said she couldn't do much for anybody, but liked to do what she could."

The Scribe : " Ever had regular work ? "

The Tramp (smiling) : " I've had one or two chances, but I don't like 'em. When I've been a week in one place I want to get to another. I've been from Yorkshire to Somerset and from Cheshire to Kent, all in a summer."

The Scribe : " What about wet weather ? "

The Tramp : " I get a sack if I can find one. That'll keep you dry for hours. And you don't catch cold when you're on the road. You get too hard for that. Never go to a spike for the night if you can help it ; you're better off in a pigsty. The pigs'd treat you kinder."

The Scribe : " What can you live on if you don't have anything given you ? "

The Tramp : " A shilling a day's plenty."

The Scribe : " Do you ever get a lift ? "

The Tramp : " Not now. Folks would up to a year or two ago. Now, if you're down and out, they think you're going to murder 'em."

The Scribe : " What made you take to the road ? "

The Tramp : " Trouble. But there, if I'd been a man o' means, I'd have tramped. I'd have been a bit more comfortable, that's all. There's a lot can't stand the life. It isn't for everybody, but if you're one of them that likes it, you can get along fine."

There we left it. I have yet to find the tramp who has a good word for the casual ward of any workhouse. There must be something wrong with many of them.

51.—SETH LAY.

" He kept it up till he got his pension," said Mrs. Drage, speaking of her father-in-law.

I had stopped to have a chat with him in the village near an old cottage of mine. Seth Lay and I were good friends. I bought hurdles from him and would watch him at work in his shed. Though he was his own master he kept strict hours, eight o'clock till one o'clock, two till six ; only on Saturday afternoons he relaxed. He made sheep hurdles for the most part about 80 inches long and almost 48 inches high, with six rails. He bought willow or ash poles from neighbouring woods where coppice was well cared for ; there was always an annual sale at one or another with a meal of bread and cheese and beer for the buyers. He split the poles with knife or mallet, skilled work indeed, and he reckoned that a hurdle took an hour and a half to make, and that half-a-dozen went to a day's work. When he was young, he told me he could make eight in a day, but that was before my time. The price of the complete hurdle varied. I have paid from fourteen to eighteen pence. In all probability his gross takings averaged fifty shillings a week or a shilling an hour, and he had to pay for his poles. He owned his cottage and brought up a large family. The village seemed empty without him ; the shed in which he worked had become a poultry house.

" He couldn't do much at it these last years," admitted Mrs. Drage. " If he got through three hurdles he was reg'lar wanked (tired). The doctor should say that was along of his heart. So now he's gone to live with Annie in th' Sheers; she kin look arter him, bein' her child'en's grown up and out to work. But she should say he ain't same as happy. He feels the miss of his shop. I went up to see him las' summer, Master Dixon was goin' nearby with a couple o' friends an' took me in his moty car an' brought me back next day; that was a mighty kind piece o' Master Dixon."

" How did you find your father ? " I asked.

" He didn't like himself any," she replied. " He should say folk don't wanter be idle after they bin workin' every day 'cept Sunday an' Christmas f'r most sixty year. ' I do hope that th' dear Lord'll find me a job o' work, time He calls me,' he sez."

Seth Lay belongs to a generation that will leave no survivors. Simple and unpretentious, he left his mark on the village, it can never be quite the same without him, at least to those of us who remember the workshop and his bench, the little stock of hurdles and the pile of ash poles. There may have been men round us who were happier and more content, but I never met any.

52.—EARLY BIRD.

The tramp sat on a stile and whittled a stick.

" You're early out," I said. " It can't be too early," he replied.

" You're a bit old for the highways," I persisted.

" Older than you think," he chuckled. " I'm a pensioner, I'm in me seventy-one."

" I'm not in the workhouse, mind ye," he went on after a pause; " I've a son-in-law. I get bed and bite in winter at his, pay me shillin' a day and do the odd jobs. But when April's half through I go."

He was a small, wiry man, grey-eyed, alert and clean; on his back a canvas bag, in his hand a strong ash stick.

We now sat on the stile side by side ; he shared my excellent sandwiches.

"Weather's the only trouble," he remarked. "Cold rain, east winds and no shelter. But give me a barn and I don't mind. It's a good life."

"Tramping ? "

"Not all the time," he said firmly. "I take days off. I can get a few odd jobs. I'm a handy man of sorts. I can put a window in or mix a bit of plaster and lay it properly, or mend broken furniture or brush a hedge or catch rats or rabbits, or double dig a garden. When weather's fine I can sleep in the open, but a few trusses of straw make the best bed."

"How many miles a day ? "

"Twenty in fair weather, but many a fine day I lay by a river bank, and sometimes I get among kind cottage folk, an' get my clothes washed for a few pence with soap and hot water."

"I can't catch colds," he told me later. "I'm too hard. I can't remember seeing a doctor, and I've all my teeth."

He had a certain pride, my passing acquaintance ; he was the master of his life. He talked in detached phrases, spreading these statements over an hour's companionship before we parted at the cross-roads and he went on his way towards a care-free summer. There was nothing in him to remind one of the down-and-out, the diseased, vicious or heartbroken whom one may meet from time to time ; men whose voice is a warning.

CHAPTER X

MAINLY ABOUT POULTRY & GOATS

53.—A Poultry Keeper.

At the corner of the lane on high ground I found Mr. Tripp surveying with unfriendly eye and disdainful expression a newly-established all-white poultry farm; it looked spick, span, and prosperous.

"A lot of new men are trying their luck with birds now-adays," I remarked.

"Drat 'em," cried Mr. Tripp. "Oughter be ashamed o' theirselves coming down here."

"Why?" I asked.

"They set theirselves up," cried Mr. Tripp passionately, "they fat their birds an' they take their eggs to market, an' we gotter look after 'em."

"What do you do to help?" I enquired.

"That ain't what I do for him," persisted Mr. Tripp, "that's what he do to me. There's a pond long side o' that old ellum tree. I go to it to water me birds, though I ain't got no more than a score nowadays. I bin to it most all me life, come the summer, to spare me pump."

"Well?" I queried.

"That ain't well," replied Mr. Tripp, "not by no means. That man's 'most run the pond dry. Morning, noon an' night he's down there arter me water; I've got to be double cunning to get my share."

"Why your water?" I asked him.

"I was born here," Mr. Tripp said with dignity, "I belong. He don't. He's come here an' he might ha' gone somewheres else. I wholly wish he had. A man shouldn't come where he hadn't oughter. I never."

I said something indistinct, conscious that I am among the offenders and have been classified.

"Too much poultry keeping," continued Mr. Tripp angrily. "A few years ago folk'd come to you an' ast f'r new laid eggs regular civil; they'd speak for a fat bird for Christmas an' time they got a birthday or a party. Nowadays they look down on powtry. They don't want a bird ne yet an egg if you haven't bin an' lost money on it. And it's folk like that," he added, pointing to the busy man fifty yards away, "what's done it. If I'd taken me bread out of a honest man's mouth I wouldn't like it," said Mr. Tripp.

"Nor would I," I said soothingly, but with genuine conviction.

54.—Modern Ideas.

Across the river, the river I know best, I had watched the work on a new poultry farm, a number of intensive houses and arks, an incubating house, a battery brooder, and all the rest of the modern equipment down to fattening pens and cramming machines. Rumour said that the three energetic men who had surrounded their bungalow with all the equipment had laid out nearly three thousand pounds. They were town folk with money and a love of the country and the simple life; they understood costings and marketing and could buy food through Mincing Lane. Business methods demanded that the incubator and the brood house with its lamp should replace the hen, and that the chicks when old enough should go to the battery brooder and be moved from one shelf to another for the minimum number of weeks, by which time the cockerels would be fit to kill and the pullets would be thinking of egg production. From birth to death the birds would be prisoners, fed on the most stimulating food and disposed of as quickly as possible because time is money. A perfect plan on paper, and carried out by keen practical men who know that birds do not need normal life and must be pushed hard to market. For a couple of years the venture had some measure of success, and then slowly but surely Nature stepped in. The laying strain and pedigree birds that had mothered or fathered the flock produced weak birds ; diseases, coccidiosis, and the other trouble known by its initials b.w.d., were followed by yet another known locally as white comb. The men from the town acted promptly and at a great loss. They scrapped the entire stock and started again with pedigree laying-strains, battery brooders and incubators and the rest. Once again Nature presented her bill and there was no answer but a sale of stock and equipment. It is well that the mongrel cocks of the old farmyard should have been replaced by something better, but light, air, and free range would appear to be Nature's price for giving us healthy birds. Since I first knew the countryside I have seen every form of production overdone in a desperate attempt to get rich quick, to make laws for Nature who, after all, can only be conquered by obedience. Soil sickness and stock sickness are the inevitable result of modern methods. It should be clear by now that Nature is not interested in money making and will not become a partner in any business that endeavours to thrive by forcing her paces. A few years before he died, Dr. Rudolf Steiner declared that, if food production was carried on in persistent defiance of natural laws, the time must inevitably come when we should starve in the midst of plenty.

"I told you they 'ouldn't come to no good," said Mr. Tripp.

"Their methods were wrong," I admitted.

" Never mind methods," replied Mr. Tripp. " Time they come stealin' my water out o' my pond I knew well enough they 'ouldn't do no good f'r theirselves. We're well riddy of 'em ; don't tell me."

55.—Confidence.

Now I record the Confident Man, alert, sandy, quick in movement and with sufficient assurance to play for England against Australia or ride in the Grand National.

" I was going up to th' house, time I see ye," he began.

" I come here to be quiet," I explained. He was altogether too dynamic for the place and the time.

The C.M. : " I've see you here one or two arternoons from across the t'other side ; that's why I come along here. I wanted to git a word with you, quite private."

The Scribe : " Well, only the birds can hear, and they're too busy just now to take much notice."

The C.M. : " It's like this here, Guv'nor. You got a nice little place for a pou'try farm."

The Scribe : " Others thought so, apparently, but they were not very successful."

The C.M. : " Lord love ye, Guv'nor, they dedn't know nawthen about it. They couldn'd ha' kep' guinea pigs. I'm giving up my farm. That ain't big enough f'r me. A thousand birds. What's that f'r a live man ? "

The Scribe (cautiously) : " A full day's work seven days a week."

The C.M. : " Not f'r me, Guv'nor. Gimme a boy an' I kin make it three thousand, an' that's MONEY. (He said it in capitals.) Six hund'ed a year profit, clear."

The Scribe : " You're sure ? "

The C.M. : " Lord love ye, Guv'nor, that's child's play. Joe Garget knows all about it. I bin keepin' buds these twenty year an' more. All you gotter do is to put down the CASH (this in capitals, too) and leave things to me."

The Scribe (hiding secret annoyance successfully) : " Quite fascinating."

The C.M. (more confidently than ever) : " I'm a gooin' to talk strite to ye, Guv'nor, that's me natur. Folk gotter trust me, or else they kin leave me alone. I can't have folk come interferin'. You gotter trust a man what works for ye, in this world. I know what I'm a dooin' on, all th' time. I kin show me papers. You gotter buy th' birds an' some new housen. Those o' yourn are all right in a way, but they ain't th' latest. You kin buy mine an' me birds, too. A thousand birds an' all me housen f'r astart, set up here out o' me own pocket. There'll be pullets an' a few score o' good layin' strain cockerels f'r breedin'."

The Scribe : " And that would cost me ? "

The C.M. : " Tharteen hundred pun an' there'd be the extry housen f'r ye to buy. But th' whole lot 'ouldn't come to two thousand from start to finish, an' there'd be six hund'ed a year in it."

The Scribe : " And what about you ? "

The C.M. : " Joe Garget don't want the arth. Give him five pun a week an' a cottage an' wegebles an' light an' firin'."

The Scribe : " But you must have a small car or a van to go to market."

The C.M. : " A van'll do. Make it a van, Guv'nor."

The Scribe (gently) : " But what about your week-ends ? You'll need a car for them if it's only a two-seater. The seaside is twenty miles away."

The C.M. (less confidently) : " I bin an' made you a fair offer, man to man, Guv'nor."

The Scribe : " I'm not saying you haven't. If you will send me testimonials from all the people who have employed you since you started, and audited accounts of your own farm showing a profit of two hundred pounds a year on your thousand birds, after allowing labourer's wages for one man— I'll think it over."

The C.M. (disillusioned and speaking with great bitterness) : " I ain't no time to waste on figures an' letters, Guv'nor. If you don't want me, there's a many do."

The Scribe (magnanimously) : " It may be their need is greater than mine. I feel it must be. Good-day."

He did respond, but I've not added his response to my record. It would not look pretty in print.

Who was he ? Whence came he ? I spoke to one or two people who know the neighbourhood but they can't place him, and since that one swift descent he has never shown himself.

56.—GEESE.

You can learn quite a lot in the country by sitting still and doing nothing, and it is hard to find a more pleasant summer-time occupation. I go to the summerhouse or to one of my little " hides " by the wood, with notebook or writing-pad and, when neither appeals, look about me quietly. If anything occurs I do as Captain Cuttle advised and make a note of it. In the past few days, while sitting in the summerhouse I have found that an expectant mother rabbit has escaped our vigilance and made her " stop " behind a wych elm. In consideration of her state, she is merely sentenced to be dug out and returned to the far side of the wire there to find another nursery. How hideously frightened she was as she lay in my arms, with wide staring eyes, her ears flat back, her heart beating hard. When I set her gently on the ground, nearly a minute passed before she could run away. Had she any premonition of disaster?

I know where a bumble bee had her home, where robin, hedge sparrow and wren nested, the trees that the green and great spotted woodpeckers turn to most readily for a meal and the oak whose gnarled front hid the tree-creeper's family. I have seen peacock butterflies past numbering, and the home of the nightingale which stayed awhile in silence on the post above a gorse spray. Apart from these discoveries, I have watched life passing round the edge of the wood, life that whether of beast, bird or insect, would seem to be brimful of happiness just now.

Further afield, and in more active mood, I have talked of geese with Mr. Studdy, smallholder and poultry-farmer, over his garden hedge ; he is one whom the buffets of the world have so incensed that he would quarrel gladly with a five-barred gate. We meet but seldom and he is always ready to express his complete disagreement with my viewpoint, whatever the matter of discussion. He puts me in the wrong and leaves me there, not out of ill-will but because his nerves need a tonic and don't get one indoors, where, if report be true, Mrs. Studdy assumes the bifurcated garment.

The Scribe (tranquilly, and pointing with approval to the geese on the meadow) : " I've a great fancy for geese. They are interesting and can be made quite tame. There are some

CHINESE GEESE

wonderful Chinese geese in England to-day. They are good to look at and lay well. I think of having a few myself."

Mr. Studdy (suspiciously) : " Chiny geese ! I ain't never heard o' sech. Do they eat tender ? "

The Scribe (frankly) : " I've never eaten them. I've only seen them."

Mr. Studdy (severely) : " You don't wanter goo to Chiny f'r geese. Chiny's a furrun part. I've read many a piece in th' paper about it. They bin fightin' there o' late seem'ly. Furriners are all alike to my thinkin'. You don't wonter to buy their geese."

The Scribe (mildly) : " You're quite right, but you can buy the geese in England ; they are bred here."

Mr. Studdy (growing angry) : " That don't sinify. If they're Chinese they come from Chiny. Can't help their-selves."

The Scribe (peacefully) : " I don't think we keep enough geese in these parts."

Mr. Studdy (sarcastically) : " The owd fox don't think so neither, I lay. But there, a goose is the same as a cow."

The Scribe (firmly) : " No, surely not. (With confidence) : I can always tell the difference ; I'll teach you if you want to learn."

Mr. Studdy (loftily persistent) : " A goose is same as a cow ; they both want a nice bite o' grass an' plenty o' clean water. Leastaways, English geese do ; I don't know nawthen about furrin birds. Never had no truck wi' sech, an' I don't want I should, t'ain't likely."

The Scribe (emphatically as he points to the Toulouse gander and geese on Mr. Studdy's pasture) : " They're from Toulouse, and Toulouse is in the south of France."

Mr. Studdy (very annoyed) : " That don't sinify nothin' to me where Toulouse is. Them geese is as English as I am an' if anybody towd me they ain't, I'd call him a liar, beggin' y'r pardon."

The Scribe (indifferently) : " They don't lay nearly so well as Chinese geese."

Mr. Studdy (coldly) : " I don't want they should. They lay well enough f'r th' likes o' me. (Passionately) : I ouldn't have a Chiny goose on my meddy if somebody bin an' pide

me to put it there.   I do wholly wonder th' p'liceman ain't
been on to ye about 'em.   (Confusedly):   Taking a livin'
outer honest men's mouths along of a lot of furriners."

I had not thought that Chinese geese could have roused so
much emotion in Mr. Studdy, but when later on I received
catalogues from gentlemen who keep these geese for sale, I,
too, was conscious of a related emotion.   It led me to consign
the price lists to the waste-paper basket.   Summer is no time
to buy store birds ; you are likely to pay in August consider-
ably more than they will be worth in November.

57.—THE KINDLY MAN.

I went far afield this afternoon, for the sun would not
suffer me to sit at my desk, and just outside a placid, sleepy
village I encountered a Kindly Man ; he has a cottage
holding and keeps goats.   At the close of a few introductory
remarks I admitted that I, too, was a cottage holder.

" What you want, guv'nor," he assured me with easy
confidence, " is a goat.   That's same as a poor man's cow."

" I've often thought about goats," I remarked truthfully
enough ; the L.A. and I once suffered from a herd of twenty-
five, and they gave us two hours' strenuous work a day."

" I got a couple o' goats that'd do credit to anybody,"
said the Kindly Man.

" Which are they ? " I enquired, looking at the poor company tethered by the roadside.

" These here, Governor," replied the Kindly Man, pointing
to a couple of large-horned, large-bodied, small-uddered
females of uncertain age, their market value when in profit
round about five shillings apiece, to all save the uninformed.

" What are they ? " I asked, well knowing there could be
no true answer to that question, since they were nondescripts.

" They're same as Noobian Toggenburgs," he assured me.
" It ain't long since a gent come past here an' offered me an
oncommon lot o' money f'r 'em, if I'd keep 'em till September.
But there, you gimme fower pun f'r th' two, an' I'll drive 'em
to yours."

Thoughts of the gent's distress when he called for his
bargain overcame me.

" No," I said.   " I can't take them from your customer.

GOAT AND KID

Why should he be disappointed? He may be looking to them
for the winter milk supply for his wife and little children.

"Well, I might let ye have one or two o' th' t'others,"
suggested the Kindly Man, "but, of course, they'd come
to more money."

"I kept goats for many years," I said suddenly, "bought
and sold them; they were bred from one of the finest sires
in England—Grange Grenadier. I've had up to a gallon a
day from the best in full milk."

"Lord, Governor," he replied. "Why didn't ye tell me
that afore I tried to put it acrost ye? But mind ye," he
added, indicating not without a certain satisfaction his
unfortunate collection, "I ouldn't call 'em a bad lot."

Now you will understand why I gave him his name. Any
but a kindly man must have called them a very bad lot indeed.

58.—POULTRY PROBLEMS.

Mr. Tope, one of the older poultry farmers near here knows his business, his speciality is a first cross for the table ; a widower, he works with his grandson.   Here is a little record of two conversations.

The Scribe : " Have you a dozen good birds four to five pounds that you can let me have at the rate of one, perhaps two, a week ? "

Mr. Tope : " I can't do that f'r ye.   Tell ye f'r why. Chickens is bound to rise.   If I ast ye to-day's price I'd be robbin' meself every week.   Everybody wants a good chicken."

The Scribe : " But prices may fall.   They do after the summer season.   London doesn't buy much after July."

Mr. Tope : " You don't want to tell me.   Prices'll be high along o' the weather we bin an' had these past years.   You'd better come here every week an' I'll treat ye fair."

The Scribe : " But will you keep the birds for me ? "

Mr. Tope : " If so be I can.   But I can't get half the birds I want.   I don't get no peace o' me life along o' folks askin' me for 'em."

A little later in the same week a man I know told me he was giving up his poultry because he is too busy to attend to them and the flock is too small to carry a paid worker. I advised him to go to Mr. Tope and offer his young table birds for finishing.   Here so far as I can gather is what Mr. Tope told him.

" Everybody's trying to sell chickens but nobody wants to see one.   They're no trade to-day.   Folk grumble at a fair price.   They'll go down every week, will chickens, mark my words if they don't.   Trade's all right up to July. After that they tell me fash'nable folk won't look at a chicken, if you were to bring it to them ready cooked.   I've more birds than I know what to do with.   But there, I'll give ten pence a pound an' I'll lose money on them, sure as harvest."

There is matter for satisfaction in the thought that one of Mr. Tope's prophecies must justify him.

CHAPTER XI

SOME OTHER LOCAL RESIDENTS

59.—RATS.

I WAS near enough to Mr. Candy to make a passing call. He had a trap in his hand and a dead rat in the trap.

"The varmint," said Mr. Candy, pointing to his victim. "Thought he'd git upsides along o' me, but he never. Now," he added, with a flash of insight, "he on't come interferin' along o' me no more!"

"They are a real trouble," I agreed.

"The trouble along of rats rightly speakin'," declared Mr. Candy, with his usual assurance, "is that they keep on keepin' on."

"The way out" I suggested "is for us to do the same."

"I count you can't," retorted Mr. Candy. "You may be cunnin' but they're double cunnin'. Why, there's a owd rat get to my corn bin reg'lar, an' I got a tin lid on't and the sides ain't bin touched."

" May I have a look ? " I said, and he took me to the shed.
The corn bin proved to be a tarred barrel. " They can't
abide tar, the mucks ! " boasted Mr. Candy. " That's why I
laid it on."

" Move it ; I'll lend you a hand," I ventured, having been
seized of a bright idea.

" You don't wanter touch th' owd bin," he objected.
" That's most full ; I ain't never shifted it. Time you got a
thing in its proper place, let it bide where it stand."

But I urged him until he gave in, and we pushed the barrel
on to its side, to find as I expected, that a piece had been eaten
out of the bottom and there was a rat-run leading into the
earth on which it rested.

" What I tell't ye ? " cried Mr. Candy, in no wise perturbed. " Double cunnin', that's what they are. You
think you got 'em, but you ain't, rightly speakin'. They're
laughin' at ye."

I suggested some poison that is harmful only to rats and is
recommended by the Ministry of Agriculture. Mr. Candy
reacted violently.

" I ain't gooin' to lay no pisen about," he declared
emphatically. " There's me brother-in-law what married me
sister an' live at Stubbin'. He pisened his rats an' killed
his chickens. Don't tell me."

Any *kudos* that I had won by finding the source of leakage
had been lost when I suggested the safe and obvious remedy.
Truth to tell I had done no more than annoy Mr. Candy and
disturb an industrious rat. The trouble is that Mr. Candy
has thousands of replicas throughout the countryside and
that most of them are convinced that they can " lay for a
rat."

Rats are stirring on my neighbour's farm ; apparently he
can't cope with them, though he keeps a careful watch ;
from time to time they seek to set up house on our side of
the still unguarded boundary. We have discovered several
lines of approach, and morning after morning these are
watched for signs of use. If there are any, the track is
followed before the day's traffic has obliterated it. So far
the invaders have been females that have retired from their

usual haunts for domestic purposes, perhaps because hungry male rats, like Saturn, will devour their own offspring. There can be no consideration for the mother rat, because rats begin to breed when four months old and if the offspring of a healthy pair were suffered to live and thrive there could be from nine hundred to a thousand within twelve months. We have to choose between destroying and being destroyed, and there is a certain grim interest in following trails which lead in nearly every instance to one of several warm and sunny compost heaps. When the run is found, the trap is set in it, head on, lightly covered and unbaited; unless you have been working in the garden it is well to rub the hands in earth, for rats are suspicious, nervous creatures enough; they cannot be otherwise considering the number of their enemies—man, dog, cat, fox, stoat, weasel, owl, snake.

If rats intrude and become " worritsome " as we say, I do not trouble any more, it suffices to walk across the wood and ask my tenant the gamekeeper to come across and help me. Until I knew him I thought that nobody could show me a rat run I had overlooked, or teach me how to catch an intruder. I had sat at the feet of the late Mark Hovell, the eminent throat surgeon who, in forgotten days, went with Morell Mackenzie to help the father of the last German Emperor. Mark Hovell, most lovable of men and a friend I can never forget, gave much of his leisure to studying the ways of rats and wrote the best book on rat destruction extant. It was my privilege to be of some help to him in its production.

But the keeper who is quite without what is called book learning has wood craft that Mark Hovell himself would have envied. He uses a long iron spoon and for the first night or two he feeds meal to the rats. In earths where they congregate he has known them attack the spoon in their haste to feed. When they are accustomed to the food, he mixes his own special poison with it and the rats eat for the last time. It all sounds cruel until you have seen what far-spread damage is wrought by rats and how merciless they are to all helpless young life. I can handle toads, hedgehogs, moles and snakes with no sense of aversion, indeed I seek to protect them, but the sight of a rat fills me with a sense of disgust.

If you can find where the rat lives and feed him with a lethal powder, there is no danger of losing dogs, cats or poultry, as there is if you set down poison baits that rats may carry away and then leave in the open.

60.—RABBITS.

We did not bar the way to neighbours' rabbits a day too soon. In the burrow on our boundary they multiplied past belief, probably by reason of the mild, sunny Spring weather; now they cover the hillside so heavily that a friend from a newspaper wanted to send a staff photographer down to take a daybreak picture of them devouring a meadow. But happily on our side the tarred iron sheets are a strong defence, and these are reinforced by buried wire; hitherto all assaults have been repulsed, for your rabbit is a clean animal and cannot face tar. Yet if they could find a gap they could ruin the work of months in a single night and leave us without redress. Their numbers have declined in the wood and one countryman says that they have poisoned themselves with the young leaves of the yellow ragwort now in full flower. Culpeper is silent; he claims no acquaintance with ragwort, and after the flowering of the charming weed rabbits did decline in numbers.

61.—HEDGEHOGS.

By the edge of a neighbouring wood are the gamekeeper's trophies, remains of stoats and weasels, two dry skins of hedgehogs. These last rattle in the wind as though protesting in the only fashion left to them against the stupidity of a judgment that condemned the wearers to death. Quite apart from its engaging habits, and the hedgehog can be tamed, it eats young rats and mice as well as slugs and beetles and is the resolute enemy of our one poisonous snake, the adder. I have never seen a fight between the two, but Brusher Mills, the snake catcher of the New Forest, who thought a dozen adders quite a poor bag for a sunny Summer day, had seen many encounters, the hedgehog being the aggressor. He told me about them more than once when we tramped the forest ways round Brockenhurst, he even showed me an adder done to death by its armoured foe. So soon as it encounters the snake, the hedgehog gives one hard bite and then rolls itself up quickly, leaving the infuriated reptile to dash vainly against the spikes. Then when the adder is exhausted the hedgehog will unroll cautiously and bite again. Two or three nips will be fatal and the victor will proceed slowly and methodically ⌐rst to chew his victim and then to devour him. One was just about to enjoy his conquest when Brusher Mills came up and carried the adder away, first to show me how the attack had been made and then to add his captive to his bag. He melted the fat and made an ointment that was full of strange virtues—if he was not mistaken.

If you look about the dry heath and bracken lands that the adder frequents you may find a dead one every now and again with just a bad bite. Something or somebody has disturbed the hedgehog and he has been unable to complete his work, for completion in this case is repletion.

The Brusher was hard to understand, he spoke indistinctly. Fairies, he assured me, had cleft his palate so that when he set out to attack the snakes they love and protect, landowners and gamekeepers might suspect his intention and drive him from their land.

"That set me against snakes," he added, "an' I've paid the fairies for what they've done to me ; now there isn't a gamekeeper for miles round who doesn't know me and treat me kindly."

Gamekeepers will tell you that the hedgehog eats eggs and this is true upon occasion, for it is omnivorous, but it can and sometimes does live upon vegetables and one may be sure that young rats make ample atonement for a few eggs, while as the hedgehog is active after dusk, he is concerned with rats, slugs, mice and beetles rather than with bird's nests. A rat will do more harm to young birds and carry off more eggs than any hedgehog. That is why those dried skins proclaim the gamekeeper's unreason.

62.—PREJUDICE.

"You don't want to feed birds," declared the wise, uninvited guest, whom I met in the meadow where he was trespassing for some purpose undivulged. Probably he had a few snares in his pocket or had been looking for places where snares might be wisely set. " Do," he went on, " an' they'll have all y'r fruit." He pointed a little scornfully to the seed boxes, the coconuts and suet balls set up on the hillside to mitigate the rigours of Winter and early Spring. " You wanter catch th' birds," he explained, " afore they do ye a mischief. They've pulled me old thatch to pieces along o' their nests." I explained that if it were not for the birds he would have no vegetables in his garden and no sound fruit on his trees ; I told him that many birds would leave fruit alone if they had all the water they need and that only a few varieties are the gardener's enemy.

" I've lived hereabouts man and boy an' me father before me an' I've allus tended a garden," was the crushing rejoinder, and he left abruptly, perhaps pleased to get away without explaining his presence ; his comment may have been designed to avoid questions. I am wondering whether it will ever be possible to persuade those who require persuasion that our birds, with few exceptions, pay handsomely for what they take.

On one of my rambles I found a dead hedgehog on the grass by the side of a garden where Mr. Candy was busy.

" How stupid it is to kill hedgehogs," I remarked.

" Stupid, ye call it, do ye ? " he answered sharply. " Well, I count you're wrong. You don't want 'em about. Nasty little spinnicks* I call 'em, so did me father."

" What harm do they do ? " I demanded.

" You'll larn that when you've had anything to do with 'em," he replied. " I ouldn't have one on 'em in my garden if that was ever so. You ast Mr. Rudge ; he lives up street. He'll tell you, and he bin a gamekeeper an' all. He'll kill one as soon as look at it."

As Mr. Candy was clearly glad to rest from his labours for a moment, I told him of tame hedgehogs I have kept and how amusing they are to watch.

" I don't want to watch no hedgepigs," he retorted, giving the little animal its country name. " I'd rather do a job of

---

*Anything small and unpleasant may be described as a spinnick but the term is generally kept for troublesome children.

work," and so saying Mr. Candy, having recovered his breath, resumed his task with a grunt of satisfaction proper to one who feels he has had the best of the encounter.

There is plenty of excuse for those who were taught as children that hedgehogs draw the milk from cows, take pheasants' eggs and commit other sins against farming and gamekeeping men, but why is the legend of their iniquity so long lived in days when observation is widespread and accurate ?

63.—The Red Squirrel.

The red squirrels will be pairing soon.   In a fork of one of the big conifers you may see the beginnings of a nest made up of sweepings from the wood—bark, moss, dead leaves, twigs, all woven or packed together to provide warmth and shelter for the babies to be expected early in June.   It is likely that the family will remain round the cottage, for one parent wintered in an elm on the edge of what we persist in calling the lawn.   Sometimes on sunny winter mornings he would come out of his shelter to enjoy a little exercise on bare branches and then, with newly acquired appetite, make way cautiously to some smaller trees on which fat is hung for hungry birds.   One morning our small household and a visitor enjoyed an unusual sight.   The squirrel came to the branch from which suet was hanging by a string and, holding on by his hind legs, tried to reach it.   He was not quite long enough, but refused to be beaten.   By skilled manipulation of his front paws he pulled the string up until the fat was within reach of his mouth.   Then he made a hearty bite turned himself the right way up, and sat on the branch for a moment.   Looking about in his usual alert fashion he became conscious of onlookers at the window ; a moment later he was over the wire and out of sight.

I have noticed that all red squirrels like meat scraps.   When working in the summerhouse in the wood, not far away from the chicken house, I have seen some that have been playing in tree tops race to ground, pick up a scrap of meat or suet in their mouths and run away again to a point of vantage, a place where they can see all round ; then they eat delicately,

THE SQUIRREL

using their fore feet.   Even the red squirrel is not altogether harmless, nesting birds could state a case against him, but then they could state an even worse case against mankind.

64.—NIGHTINGALES.

There is a wood ten miles from here, approached by way of remote Suffolk lanes that seem to connect nowhere with nowhere by a link of wild flowers and bird song.   As a rule they are free from traffic, nothing more formidable than a farm cart is met from end to end and when you reach the unproclaimed sanctuary by way of a common golden with gorse and broom, you find that the nightingales are not concerned in any way with such poor things as human beings.   They sing to their mates and against their rivals with complete disregard for strangers ; you can approach within twenty yards if you are reasonably quiet.

One fine May day when we went to the wood we had forgotten that it was a Sunday afternoon and that rumour of the nightingales' achievement had spread through the remote countryside. There were six or seven motor cars by the entrance to the woods and on the common where the gorse and broom were flowering quite a number of very young people playing games with as much noise as seemed necessary or perhaps a little more. Even nightingales cannot stand for this, they gave no performance.

Later that evening we strolled down the meadow by the side of our own wood and there, just over the bank, two or three nightingales were in full song behind a crab-apple tree, a mass of blossom and music because every foraging bee appeared to be singing her song of content.

A few summers ago we listened over the wireless to the nightingales that visit the woods round Pangbourne and, without any wireless aid, heard them on another occasion in Maidenhead thicket. We need not travel far to-day, the birds favour us and we are grateful. But only a few miles away there is a corner that I have named the Valley of Nightingales, and well within hearing of their song Mrs. Bill (I don't know her surname) dwells in great unease. She is of limited height and of generous girth; she gardens, she takes in washing, and is said to " keep herself to herself." Is it pride or exclusiveness that makes two country people out of three claim to do the same? But be that as it may, Mrs. Bill has trusted me; she confessed her great trouble when I paused to pass the time of day and ask for a certain short cut.

" I can't abide them nightingales," she began. Such a grievance has a certain quality; it is uncommon and shared by few.

I expressed a sympathy that was insincere, even hypocritical.

" Time they come acrost here first, they ain't too bad," continued Mrs. Bill, leaning on her garden gate, " but afore April's hardly over they keep on keepin' on, an' then you can't git no peace of your life."

" I bin down me back garden on'y th' night afore last," she went on with a sudden accession of anger, " to shoo one off o' th' holly tree at the end. I might ha' caught me

THE NIGHTINGALE

death o' cold but that wouldn't ha' mattered, I lay.   There's
whiles I don't git a wink o' sleep.   Most all th' other birds
about here are right enough.   They start shouting early,
but I don't mind that, come a fine morning.   It's them
nightingales what pleg me.   They dedn't oughter be allowed."

"There are people who will travel miles to hear nightingales," I urged, just to give her a fresh viewpoint.

"They don't wanter travel so far, leastways not if they
live round here," retorted Mrs. Bill, tossing her head to
emphasise contempt for fellow creatures.   "Let 'em come
hereabouts, and if they're that fond o' nightingales they can
take 'em back where they belong an' welcome.   I kin spare
'em.   Aggravatin' creatures ever I listened to."

"When we come here first an' I'd had me first taste of
'em," she went on, "I sez to me husban', ' Bill,' I sez, ' we
don't wanter stop.'   But Bill's that deaf he can't hear nothin',
so he should ha' said he dedn't wanter goo.   That's just like
a man, he just sez if we moved that'd be ill convenient for
his work.   This is a pore place to live in 'twixt late April
an' middle June, I kin tell ye."

"Perhaps you don't care for birds?" I ventured.

"I like 'em in their proper place," protested Mrs. Bill, "so long as they're natural. There's my gel Minnie what's married an' live at Clacton. She got a canary an' that kin sing be the hour. But time Minnie bin an' put the duster on the cage that'll be as quiet as a mouse till she take it off. A bird don't wanter sing all night, time folk wanter mite o' rest. It aint respectable."

"But, there, you goo down the lane an' askew the meddy by th' footpath an' then first on th' left'll take you to the main road. I hope you don't get th' nightingales where you belong."

65.—A TOAD.

This afternoon, down by the little brook in a warm and protected corner, a slight disturbance by the bank, a movement among grasses, revealed a toad, most welcome of visitors, early out. He is now in the cold greenhouse where perhaps grubs and worms stirred by the gardener's fork may tempt him to remain. It is possible to persuade a toad to feed out of your hand; you may draw him to your side on a summer evening with lure of music from gramophone or wireless, particularly if either should carry the human voice. Long years ago, before gramophone was popular or ether had been harnessed, a toad would come to the garden night after night to hear the singing which filled a part of our leisure hours. He would waddle as far as the porch, stay contentedly and slip away soon after the last song was sung. Year after year he came; everybody was invited to walk warily past the porch. Following full summer he would disappear, to return to the near orchard on early autumn afternoons, sit under the alighting board of a hive, and snap up late foragers that paused within reach of his very active head. The position was delicate. We could not persecute our friend of summertime, nor could we suffer tired bees to be devoured. So the toad would be picked up and carried courteously to a far meadow.

"You don't want to handle an' owd toad, Master," said a countryman who met me on one of these journeys; "do, he'll sting ye with his tongue, an' that's pisen. Set him down and I'll treed on him f'r ye." He took a long time to forgive me for pretending to know more than he did about " owd toads."

66.—A Country Conversation.

First Small Rabbit (crouching on grass patch inside the wire to still smaller rabbit beyond) : " You can get through if you like, but see you've a clear way out, you may need it."

Second Small Rabbit (pricking up his ears) : " What's the trouble ? Stoats, weasels, snakes ? "

First S.R. : " No, we haven't any here, but there's a man with a dog in the summerhouse."

Second S.R. (nervously) : " What happens if he sees you ? "

First S.R. : " He just stares as if he'd never met a rabbit in his life, but if the lurcher's looking she's away before you can turn round. If she catches you she may pick you up in her mouth and take you to him. She did that to me."

Second S.R. (breathlessly) : " What happened ? "

First S.R. : " He put me over the hedge and told me to run away and stay away, but I'm not taking any more risks. He may be hungry another time. He keeps all the green things inside there for himself though he never eats them. I don't know what he finds to live on." (Resumes meal.)

(Second rabbit goes back quietly.)

Two cock blackbirds fly on to a branch in front of the summerhouse. Their tails are up, their wings are spread, they are excited.

First C.B. : " You've no right in that corner ; I'm living there with my family."

Second C.B. : " I'll go where I like. Do you want to fight ? "

First C.B. : " Yes." (They attack one another and disappear fighting.)

Enter certain finches, very excited. They perch on the long branch of a chestnut tree and all talk at once.

A Chaffinch : " What with hawks, jays and owls, life's a burden."

Wood Pigeon from fir tree top) : " You've nothing to grumble about. There's a partridge nest in the grass by the rhododendron on the top of the bank and Mrs. Partridge tells me a hedgehog comes every morning early and takes one of her eggs. She's helpless."

A Greenfinch (enviously) : " Well, you're safe ; nothing can reach you ! "

Wood Pigeon : " Except the men with guns. I'm afraid to cross the meadows, you never know where trouble is coming from. They wouldn't fire at you, you're too small. Look out, there's a jay coming."

Jay flops heavily down on the floor of the wood. She flies to a hedgesparrow's nest and finds it empty, looks up and sees that she is being watched from the summerhouse, protests harshly and flies away.

Mr. Wood Pigeon (to his wife) : " Why can't the horrid thing leave small birds alone ? I've watched him make a good many meals of worms and grubs, so there's plenty for him without birds."

Mrs. Wood Pigeon (indifferently) : " Coo. Coo."

A green woodpecker dashes into the wood and makes for her nest, a hole scooped out of the trunk of an elm tree, twenty feet above the ground ; the chips are still lying on the grass.

Thrush (looking up from her nest in elder bush, to her partner, who is perching nearby) : " That's the sort of home to have."

(She crouches hurriedly on her brood for a sparrowhawk has followed close on the woodpecker, drawn by the bright colouring. He tries to strike woodpecker, but in vain. The bird is too quick and runs round the trunk using feet as skilfully as if he lacked wings, the hawk is only able to save himself by a prodigious flutter.)

Sparrowhawk (out of breath) : " I'll have you."

Green Woodpecker (looking round corner of the trunk and quite at his ease) : " Ha, ha ! You think so ! "

Sparrowhawk dashes at him twice, but Woodpecker is too nimble and the hawk leaves hurriedly in what may be in bird-land a towering rage. Woodpecker waits for a few minutes and then flies for some very old trees across the meadow screaming as he flies, just as if his fear had found sudden voice.

Wood being quiet now, a blackbird gives a recital.   There is an undertone of critical comment, chiefly from finches and a long-tailed tit.   They haven't a song between them to rival the singer and they know it.   A spotted flycatcher comes to rest on the top strand of wire and waits.   Foolish flies and other winged insects enjoy the summer afternoon.   Flycatcher jumps up when they are within striking distance, to swallow them and return to his perch.   At this season his food stores are all round him and they could not be more fresh.

Enter from the meadow large and ugly cuckoo of tender years with two hedge sparrows in attendance.   He takes his place on the spreading branch of an ash.   The two foster parents get busy, returning several times in a minute with insects for their foster child who is larger than the two of them together.   " Hurry up, I'm hungry ! " he cries incessantly. He does not take the trouble to watch their hard labours, is content to open his mouth that they may fill it.

" Coming, sonny," they reply

While they are both collecting, a hen cuckoo slips through the trees in curious hawk-like flight and utters a burbling note that the younger cuckoo ignores.   By the time one of the hedge sparrows returns, hen cuckoo has gone.   Was she the mother ?   The man asks the lurcher what she thinks.   Lurcher wags tail in fashion utterly non-committal ;   she has no opinion, but likes to be consulted.   He has met people very much like her.

Red squirrel jumps lightly from a Scotch fir to a spruce, choosing a moment when the sun has conquered some clouds. The effect is startling, the coat of the newcomer glows as though dipped in gold.   He looks down on the hut with a curious mixture of curiosity and suspicion, runs round the trunk and has another look, keeping most of his body concealed and only showing the small inquisitive head with its pointed ears.   Then he slips down to the floor of the wood to pick up meat scraps from the chicken's bowl.   A minute later he had disappeared, the young cuckoo has flown away, the blackbird is silent, only the flycatcher remains at work. All is quiet again.   A mole in the little garden of the wood becomes suddenly active and moves along close to the surface, making a track that is plainly visible.   The lurcher sees the movement, she cannot possibly have heard it, and pounces, but happily her energy is wasted ; the mole has gained depths and safety ; not all the moles that Nellie detects have the same good luck.   Now she returns looking foolish.

From a neighbouring tree comes a hissing sound, the squirrel had not gone far, and has seen the dog.

" Ugly, useless beast," he cries, but the lurcher is too proud to reply to mere abuse.

A pheasant flies across the valley, lights on the pine needles, calls loudly and runs fast into cover, for no manifest reason. Another cock pheasant sees him from some brushwood twenty yards away and advances to the attack.   These birds are at least a year old, perhaps two.   They have run every risk from the time they were chicks, indeed, even when they were eggs.   Now they might be enjoying a few months of peaceful life, but they attack one another so furiously that I have to stand up and shout, when they fly different ways. It is a brief respite, I'm afraid ; you can pick up a dead or injured pheasant now and again during the spring months, and so can a fox.

A pair of chaffinches complete with fully-fledged young family play round a big elder.   Silence becomes so deep that the pigeons in the Scotch fir feel that they must break it and their note sets the mood of the moment to music.

On the edge of the wood where the ground dips, a clump of white campion and pink ragged-robin is stirred by some stealthy passage, perhaps a hen pheasant piloting her young brood, perhaps a hedgehog.

The tree-creeper that has a nest under the bank of the old elm tree has come out in search of an early supper.   He runs up the trunk searching all the time and taking an insect or two in his stride, spreads his tail fanwise when he stops, having gone as high as he wishes, then flies down and climbs again.   There are two or three rotten trees in that corner and the creeper works each in turn, but every now and again can be seen mounting with a slower movement that looks stiff and mechanical. He rests on his tail when the nightingale comes out of the thornbush, looking very sleek and self-satisfied.

" Hullo ! " says the tree-creeper. " You've given up making a noise at last. Some of us can get a little sleep at night now."

" If you've a family and work all day to keep their mouths filled you're too tired to sing when the night comes," replies the nightingale. " Five of them, all eating their heads off," and so saying he moves off half fluttering, half flying in search of insects. He would be ashamed to confess that his wonderful voice began to fail about the time the cherries ripened, and will soon have disappeared ; he must go to the south and come back again to find it.

A gunshot rings out and is followed by another. A few moments later the keeper comes along the ride, gun under arm and carrying a pair of stoats by the tail. " I've been waiting for them most an hour," he remarks. " I'm going to tie them up."

The man does not know whether to be glad or sorry. They were born killers and did no more than exercise their function, but there will be rabbits and mice and young birds that will be the happier since the cartridges served their purpose. The shots have had a curious effect upon the wood. The undertone of song is silenced, even the pigeons are still.

ELM TREE STRUCK BY LIGHTNING

CHAPTER XII

THE IMPORTANCE OF TREES

67.—AN ELM.

WHILE the old elm stood alone in its summer beauty no man regarded it. When the lightning chose it for target, ripping the mighty trunk from crown to bole, folk came along to stare and make comment wise or foolish.

"Have you seen the old ellum?" enquired Mr. Tripp; it is not more than a quarter of a mile from his cottage.

"That's a mercy," he continued when I nodded, "Master Stint's sheep weren't in the meddy. That's the headest tree; they'd ha' gone under it sure as harvest, and the old lightning would have got the lot and not a penny for Master Stint. If Govinment did the right thing by folk, that'd pay for lightnin'."

"Perhaps," I admitted a little diffidently, for I was not so sure as he is.

"There's no perhaps about it," retorted Mr. Tripp sharply "There's me old Uncle Jonas; dead afore you come down here. A good farmer was Uncle. He could fat a beast alongside of anybody. The year before he died the lightning got at one of the bullicks he was getting ready for the Show. And nobody paid him a penny piece. That poor thing stood under a tree in a storm, never knew any better."

"No tree's safe in a storm," I suggested.

"A thorn's all right," said Mr. Tripp. "Anybody will tell you that. You never heard of anybody being struck under a maythorn. All other trees are tricky and the ellum's the worst of the lot. If lightning doesn't hit it an ellum will throw a branch, time you're passing, out of mischief. That's the mos' unfriendly tree in the world is the ellum."

"Some say the ash is the tree that attracts lightning," I reminded him and he was annoyed.

"If I troubled myself about what some say," he retorted, "I'd have nothing else to do. I could leave me garden to

look after itself.   But I ought to know.   It wasn't an ash
that drew the lightning to Uncle's bullick.   If it had been,
that bullick would have gone to the Show, for there wasn't
an ash in the field.   And if there'd bin a thorn and the
bullick bin an' laid down under that the lightning couldn't
have got near it.   Don't tell me.   You want a maythorn
in the garden an' house-leek on th' roof.   Then you're
safe."

How many centuries must have passed since these beliefs
came first into England?   In all probability the Druids knew
all about them.   And how long have we to go before urban-
isation, changing the face of fashion of our countryside, buries
the last of these beliefs under the foundations of desirable
villas complete with modern conveniences to be bought on the
instalment system together with the furniture and the motor
car and the anxiety that comes with credit.

Mr. Tripp is a storehouse of old beliefs, prejudices and
superstitions; that is why I like to visit him.

68.—WOODCRAFT.

The great boughs of the elm trees are things of beauty
but they are not a joy for ever, in spite of statement to the
contrary by John Keats.   When I saw the top branches of
the elm tree turn brown I began to look out for trouble, when
an owl made her home in one of the hollows, I knew the
time for action had arrived.   So ropes, chains and ladders
were called for and two sturdy workers climbed up to rope
limb to limb, tie subtle knots and use sharp saws.   I imagine
it would be hard to watch a surgical operation without deep
interest and this manipulation of old elms is no less.   Some of
the spreading branches overhung a glass house, others
threatened the newly-laid ground that we call a lawn when
nobody is present to contradict us.   And through the brief
hours of a late autumn day ropes and chains, ladders and
saws were busy, the gradual growth of many years came
away gently and slowly, always in the required direction.
Never a pane of glass was touched, even the rabbit netting
escaped intact, and though huge limbs lay on the " lawn,"
they were not there for long.   White elm has at least one

quality, it burns well and does not crackle and splutter as some of the woods round us will.

The workmen, taking well-earned tea in the kitchen, congratulated one another on a neat job, and not without justification; logs were piled, some served the stove I sit before throughout the winter; a menace has been removed, very little examination sufficed to show how real it was. But the garden is the poorer and if anybody should praise it in years when part of our dreams have come true, I shall hear myself saying: " You should have seen it before the old elms were topped. It has never been the same since."

After all, if you reach the time when the past holds so much more than the future can, and I hope this may be your position some day, you will talk in this fashion.

I remember that my grandfather did, so did my father and so do I. And we, in talking of the countryside at least, shall be justified of the memories that are in us. In this latest place of sojourn, we have dwelt only a few years, but within a three-mile radius I could show you at least a hundred bungalows, the most of them complete with aspidistra between the lace or cotton curtains of its sitting room window. The vulgarising or suburbanizing of our countryside develops at an incredible pace and woe to the tree that stands in the way of the speculative builder. It will not be lopped or trimmed, it will be cut down and the roots will be drawn from their shelter, in many cases a shelter centuries old.

69.—TIMBER.

There is not much thrill to be found in the builder's yard when you wish to select timber, but there is real pleasure in a visit to the cottage and outbuildings by the side of an old wood where carpenter and assistants work in open air and fair weather holds the land in its pleasant keeping. I wanted gate posts, of the kind that should be standing when our grandchildren are old; I sought the man who looks after a neighbour's woodlands. His *fiat* is enough to bring century-old oaks, broad chestnuts, and stately sycamores crashing to the ground, to be topped, lopped, trimmed and finally drawn on a limber by a team of sturdy horses to a workshop in the shadow of trees that were near neighbours of the mighty fallen.

The woodman who has grown grey at his job, will tell you all about the nature of timber, the value and right variety of coppice, the purposes that are best served by any tree. Whether it is the oak for gates and gateposts, the ash for hurdles, the chestnut for pales, or the special blue variety of white willow that makes our cricket bats, he knows all about defects and excellencies ; his advice is sound.   To him every tree has its quality, each is as much to him as pedigree farm stock is to its owners ; he knows their points as a farmer knows those of a cow.   Sit on the trunk of a felled oak and start tree talk while the birds are singing all round you and the loose-strife has coloured the woodland floor ; you will lose all thought of time, you will have some of the joy of the country that still lingers in its byways, the joy that no casual visitor savours.

70.—The Crab Apple.

The crab apple down in the meadow is so beautiful an ornament to the wood that all neighbouring tree lovers should be daily visitors in blossoming season, just as I am.   As I came from enjoying its radiant colour and joyful music, an elderly ploughman, my near neighbour, was in the lane.   He is to be envied, though he is quite unaware of this.   He has passed the allotted span, enjoys his old age pension and can do a day's work with plough or harrows, clean a ditch, brush a hedge, tend a horse and enjoy God's sunshine as though he were a child.   Indeed he has never lost a certain simplicity that goes with the golden age.

" That's a rare beauty," he said.   " Our finest sight," I replied.   " Just now I can't have too much of it."   " Glad you're pleased," he went on.   " I did the planting."

" Tell me all about it," I asked him.

" Like this," he replied.   " They were laying out this wood then, thirty year or so ago, and I was helping.   I knew where there were some slips of crab apple so I brought them along and planted them on the brow of the ditch, because the crab likes moist soil and a bit of good earth. Up there where the pines stand would have been too light. I tended them slips awhile till they were able to fend for themselves and they've grown as you see." He puffed at his pipe, well pleased.

Think, those of you who have made or written music, books or plays, have painted pictures, followed handicrafts, done anything in short to leave a little memorial in the form of beauty in the world where "fame like a dome of many coloured glass, stains the white radiance of eternity." Pause for a moment. Whether you have succeeded or failed, striven or merely dreamt of striving, ask whether you can challenge the achievement of this unlettered husbandman who was toiling for the barest approach to living wage, in a world that boasted few of its modern wonders. To-day, an old man, he has provided his own memorial, and in a fashion that evades definition he knows the truth and is content. The long day is done and he is for the night, but in that day he has kept a corner of the world clean and productive, has enjoyed good health and planted a tree that will be a joy to the eye.

"I kep' me wife mos' fifty year," he said to me once (he is a widower), "an' we nearly allus had enough to eat an' a bit o' firin' come the winter. Times worn't so easy for folk as they are now, but there, if you look at things straight, there's allus somethin' to be grateful for. I've never wanted a doctor all me born days, an' I got all me teeth an' I kin keep 'em busy."

71.—OBSTINACY.

"What you bin a doin' on up at yours?" enquired Mr. Tripp when I saw him last. I told him. He has never paid me a visit, though not for lack of invitation.

"You don't want to goo worritin' about all those tifflin' (trifling) things," said Mr. Tripp. "I never. A man want to grow what he kin eat and what'll be ready time he wants it."

I pointed to the great ash tree that shadows Mr. Tripp's cottage.

"Somebody did that for you," I remarked.

"I lay they never," replied Mr. Tripp decisively. "That

wore a big tree, time me father worn't no more than a boy. The man what planted that never set eyes on me."

"We must think of those who will come after us," I urged, "and give them a beautiful countryside to live in."

"That's a rum 'un," replied Mr. Tripp quite unconvinced. "Whatever we got to do that fower? Can't they look arter theirselves same as we got to?"

"Do you?" I queried. "Somebody planted that tree and the holly hedge and somebody dug your well."

"Time I come inter these parts I got to double dig every rod o' me garden an' buy me seeds," persisted Mr. Tripp, content to ignore wells and holly hedges. "Time I started me chickens I got to buy a old hen an' a settin' of eggs. Nobody done nothin' f'r me."

"But we have to think of those who follow us," I persisted.

"I lay we haven't," said Mr. Tripp. "We don't owe 'em nothin'. We couldn't, by th' good rights," he explained with a flash of inspiration, "bein' they ain't here."

"We must help one another," I said firmly. "Those who are here and those who are coming, those who are babies now."

"I ain't agin that," replied Mr. Tripp. "You bin tellin' me as how you're gooin' to keep all y'r best seed. Do ye bring me a few early peas an' a few good broad beans time you got 'em nice an' dry, an' when the right time comes I'll let you have some of the best white currants ever you tasted. There ain't nobody round here kin grow 'em same as I do, though there's a many fancies they can, the spufflers. You don't wanter bother about the babies what got to grow up," he concluded with decision. "They can't look arter gardens, little mucks, an' time they're old enough they'll steal y'r fruit if you was th' p'liceman hisself."

So saying, Mr. Tripp dismissed me to my labours and resumed his own.

72.—THE PEAR TREE.

In a valley a few miles off, if you measure by crow's flight, but many miles if you must go down the estuary and across the bridge and along the far side of the river, there stands a noble pear tree, a William. It was covered with bud and blossom and I thought of the quince stocks waiting their hour on a strip of rich land above Black Brook. " Mr. Flint, Bespoke Bootmaker," ran the legend, and in the garden was the familiar notice " Tea's," most favoured country spelling of the alluring word.

Mr. Flint was not making or mending boots—he was following Adam's occupation industriously. When I bade him " Good afternoon," he relaxed and stood up, so far as a shoemaker can—a clean-shaven, elderly man, blue-eyed and shrewd, and slightly suspicious of the stranger.

" A fine day, sir."

Mr. Flint nodded agreement.

" I've lost one of the metal lace holders on my boot," I began, " and a rubber heel is loose ; can you help me ? "

" Happen you'll come along in," suggested Mr. Flint, and I followed him to what had once been a fowl-house and is now a workshop. There the missing holder was replaced and the heel made secure. " That'll be fowerpence," said Mr. Flint in a tone that indicated resolution, and having paid I followed to the garden.

" That's a wonderful pear tree," I remarked.

" She's the headest pear tree in these parts, though I sez it," Mr. Flint assured me. " She's a masterpiece, that's what she is. I count she'll want a mite o' thinnin'."

" Perhaps you would sell me a few spurs later on, towards the end of June ? " I suggested, and Mr. Flint came to attention as a good terrier does when his master says " rats."

" I've had folk ast me to sell 'em pears," he remarked suspiciously, " but I ain't never sold no branches to nobody. That'd be a rum thing to do, to my thinkin'. I doubt I ouldn't like to do a thing like that."

" I only want a dozen," I urged, " and I'd give you a shilling for them."

" Would ye now ? " replied Mr. Flint, a far deeper suspicion in his regard. " Whatever d'ye want 'em fower ? "

" Does that matter ? " I asked him.

" Folk buy pears to eat, by th' good rights," replied Mr. Flint severely. " There's whiles they buy 'em f'r to make perry, though that's a messy drink to my thinkin'. But they don't wanter buy a man's buds off o' his trees."

" Why not ? " I enquired.

" That ain't done," declared Mr. Flint. " Leastaways not by right for'ard folk. It ain't seemly. You dedn't come all over here where you don't belong f'r to get a rubber nailed on," he added, as the light dawned. " That would have held awhile rightly speakin'. That'd ha' took ye back where you come from. Come over here along o' me owd tree, I doubt."

" No," I assured him, " it was quite by chance."

" Happen you're tellin' me th' truth," said Mr. Flint, " an' happen you ain't. But I ain't sellin' no pear tree branches to nobody, t'ain't likely. Time my father was alive th' Wise Woman what lived up th' Endway asked him to let her have hazel wands an' he ouldn't do it. He dedn't want to help folk to do other folk a mischief, an' no more don't I. Come along time they're ripe an' I'll sell ye a stone or two an' ast ye a fair price : nobody can't hurt nawthen with them."

" Do you take me for a Wise Man," I asked severely, and Mr. Flint was very clearly perturbed.

" I ain't said so," he replied guardedly, even nervously. " I'm a man what lives peaceable. I don't goo makin' enquirations. I don't goo interferin' wi' folk. I keep meself to meself."

Thereupon Mr. Flint retired hastily to his little shop and closed the door and I knew full well that he would not leave it until he thought the coast was clear.

Hazel wands were used against Wise Men and Wise Women in the old days, they made houses safe from the evil eye. In cottages along the estuary many years ago, I have seen them nailed over the front and back doors. Clearly Mr. Flint believed that I wanted his pear buds for unlawful ends, for magic, in fact, and indeed I did. There is something of magic in the transformation that ensues when quince stock and pear bud meet under wise direction. There will be buds available in the near future, all being well, but Mr. Flint's fine pear tree will not renew its youth on the hillside above Black Brook. The pity of it.

Belief in witchcraft lingers in Essex and East Anglia. The panel doctor has done more than anybody to kill it because he has brought medical aid within the reach of all. In the old days the country folk would rather pay a shilling to a Wise Woman than half-a-crown to a registered practitioner, and more often than not the Wise Woman was a herbalist with knowledge of the medicinal value of certain common herbs. I knew one who claimed acquaintance with what she called " them stars an' planits " and would leave her clients in her kitchen with large horse skull on the dresser while she went into the garden to take stellar instruction. So soon as she had been told what to do, she would give the sufferer a cup of her extract of " herbs o' healin'." She stewed various leaves and strained the brew, adding sugar and ginger, and the brew cured every complaint from T.B. to varicose veins ; she said so, and who could have known better? Only in the most remote corners of England could you hope to find a Wise Man or Wise Woman to-day, and if you did you would find that they are called in now to advise about sick animals on farm or in house.

But the belief in their powers has survived their passing for it was born in far off centuries when what we call witchcraft was practised and it was a bitter experience for a woman to be left in her old age without a family to protect her if she were bent, withered and ill-favoured. The cry of " witch " might be enough to bring about her destruction.

Only a couple of hundred years ago scores of women were condemned to death for witchcraft at the Assize Court of this county in a single summer. It was sufficient to be poor, old and ugly and to have a few enemies. To-day we do not speak of wizards or witches, but if you listen, you may still hear of wise men, wise women, and folk " you don't want to cross."

RHODODENDRONS IN THE WOOD

CHAPTER XIII
SUMMER-TIME

73.—MIDSUMMER DAY.

JUNE holds her Midsummer Court by meadow and stream, in wood and spinney. Before five o'clock in the morning the sun has summoned her courtiers, seventeen hours later when midnight is only two hours away, the nightjar who has been brooding two eggs in the bracken is still flitting round the boles of oak and beech uttering eerie, vibrant music, while from an adjacent wheat field the corncrake fills semi-darkness with a rasping cry. Through the quiet days of middle week visitors remain afar, but the watcher who sits in the shadow of the great cherry tree is soon aware of the most significant aspects of the season.

All bird life that chance and evil accident have spared, and none can say how heavy the toll has been, is learning how to meet its needs. Oppressors, jays and magpies and jackdaws, have contrived to keep some nests out of sight and are now teaching their full-fledged young to follow the family tradition. So too are harmless finches and warblers; you can hear an undertone, the anxious chattering of parents, the response of little ones. To the listener there is something almost human about the subdued utterances often behind the thick leaf screen that June has woven for Midsummer, and this may well be, for after all it is the expression of mother love and every mother knows of the danger that threatens on all sides.

I think there is one discontented bird at least within a few yards of my quiet corner. He is the nightingale; if you will search carefully, his nest can be seen rather low in the great holly bush. There were moonlit hours in late April and May when he seemed to share the world with his rivals, the nightingale that nests in the swampy stretch of broom and gorse just beyond the wood, the two others that have made homes across the valley. Now the season of wooing and mating is over, the young are fledged and the song has gone. Nothing is left but a harsh note quite divorced from music, it was just audible a moment ago. Another visitor whose incessant call passes is the cuckoo, he and his wife have taken their responsibilities lightly but not so easily as many suppose. I know of two young birds being brought up, one by a pair of whitethroats, another by two anxious robins. As they sit on posts in the meadow and cry for food, there can be no mistake about the cost of their keep. Often unseen, though never far away, one or other of the parent birds has been watching and soon now they will be leaving their young to follow and seek the chances of the road. Faintly across the fields I hear the changing note, high up above me swifts scream or larks pour out their song.

There is a festival of colour and music, the colours we disregard as well as those we prize, the splendid variety of rhododendrons, the glorious monotony of buttercups, the blood red of poppies. And in the wood itself? There are stately foxgloves, sometimes fringing beds of bracken ; where they cluster one hears the bumble bees as they bury themselves in every open flower. Field rose and dogrose have returned, bind-weed in earliest bloom, late bluebells, honeysuckle scattering fragrance all round, ragged robin, moon daisies, a bewildering galaxy. It is hard to turn back in thought to three months ago when daffodils were proclaiming Spring, and with peaches, mock currant and forsythia gave the garden its colour, while roses were showing no more than early leaves.

Across the streamlet, only just visible by the aid of field glasses, a moorhen guides babies over shallow water that the geese have freed from weeds of all kinds. The presence of these balls of black fluff is a tribute to our efforts to keep rats down, they are a moorhen's worst enemy. The flags have yellow flowers, yellow, too, is the colour of the agrimony by the wood's edge.

Hay making is late. Fields lie deep under the grass and in that grass there is still more bird life ; partridges and pheasants are hiding their young, so are sky-lark and wood-lark. They are screened from sparrowhawk and kestrel, from hungry owls, even stoat and weasel may well be baffled. If it were not for the protection of long grasses the mortality in bird-land would be far higher than it is now. Yet a little while and the tractor-drawn cutter will take wide swathes in its stride, all the secret places of grassland will be laid bare and there will be nothing left save the corn which has another few weeks of life. It is a race against time but when all the land is cleared, the pheasants should be able to look after themselves in woodland and the partridges on stubble.

There are spaces of silence, vast spaces that the woodpecker likes to fill; I see him now and again. He wears a dark green suit and bright red crown, he mocks at stillness as he flies. Sometimes I can hear him tapping, the wood holds many old trees. His cousin, the great spotted variety, is more shy, more hard to see, but I hear him through the day among the high branches. Above the tapping, wood-pigeons, brooding in untiring domesticity, seem to be asking woodpeckers to be quiet and not to frighten their babies.

Serenity and stillness, bird and insect song, one might think that in these long almost languorous June days here at least was peace, but the idea is misleading. In the course of a stroll to the seat from which I watch wild life I have seen two little heaps of feathers. Two birds, finches both, have been struck down and the bodies carried away to where hungry flesh-eating fledglings waited. Perhaps some nests will have lost their support and small birds must die. Suffering, now as always, is as shadow to sunshine in the woodland, but the thick leafage, the masses of flowers and flowering shrubs on all sides serve to hide ugliness. Over the innermost tragedies, June and Midsummer have conspired to drop their veil so that the careless observer may think all is well. Life dominates death, save in the insect world where all manner of winged things pay toll to insect-eating birds. Size is the basis of our judgment; if only the insects were fully visible, if we could grasp the significance of the sweeping flights of swallow, martin, swift, the ceaseless work of finches and warblers, blackbird and thrush, we should understand. We are spared all this sense of destruction and see just the vivid movement of pursuit. And perhaps on this account the Masque of Midsummer compels the watcher to look on the bright side of life, to pay his little tribute of gratitude for light, colour and music, to understand that the countryside stands on the summit of achievement and that the supreme hour has arrived.

We shall have no shorter nights, no longer days ; the tide of passion that filled our little world with melody is at the flood.   There is magic in this quiet corner.   Given a book. a writing pad, the simplest meal, and one can be intensely happy from the time the dew has left the earth down to the hour when it returns.   There are only a few days in which one may feel so content to be alone in the world.   I know I shall return to them in memory when birds are silent and woods are bare.

Happily one cannot believe to-day that such a season can exist in any future however distant.   Experience has nothing to teach us when we don't desire to be taught.   And who would wish to spoil the Midsummer festival by brooding over the laws that are Nature's and beyond either understanding or amendment ? Sufficient for the day the warmth and sunshine thereof.

74.—BEE MUSIC.

The deep quiet of a Suffolk lane was disturbed suddenly by a sound I had not heard since the years before the last war, the sound of bee music.   I made for it and discovered a bee-keeper hitting the back of a frying pan with a latchkey. " Where have they gone ? " I asked him.   He pointed to a crab-apple tree on the edge of a copse only thirty or forty yards away and continued to make the familiar noise.

" They're out of reach, little varmints," he went on.   " I'll need me ladder and a skep and a cloth."

" Let me take something for you," I suggested.   Thereupon he gave up music-making, handed me the straw cover and a piece of table cloth that had seen better years, while he took a ten-stave ladder and went off to the tree where the late swarm was still gyrating.   Some little time must pass before he could hope to take it. So he set the ladder in position and came away.

" Why the kettle and pan ? " I asked him. " Do you really think the bees bother about them ? "

" No," he replied, " I don't, no more did my father.   But when I was a boy there were a dozen beekeepers about here and the music told everybody that one of us had a swarm and was following it.   We all helped one another then."

" And to-day ? "

" There's nobody to help anybody," he replied.   " I'm the only bee-keeper hereabouts.   I suppose it's habit that makes me call out after a swarm."

" Do you use any of the old straw skeps ? "

" No," he replied.   " I only keep a couple for swarms or in case I run short of a bar frame hive, but they were the best and the healthiest.   Bees wintered well and didn't waste. When I was a boy there were bee gardens all round the village, gardens with the flowers bees liked best ; now there isn't one to be seen.   It's lucky for me that there are still some small orchards and plenty of sainfoin and white clover. When you've those, you can grow what you like.   I just grow a few herbs.   I wholly wonder why more folk don't keep bees."   I looked hard at him and saw that though advanced in years he stood upright and that his hands were supple.   " No rheumatism ? " I ventured, and he laughed.

" That's right," he replied, " and you never met a seasoned beekeeper who had."

I had to agree.   As one of the honourable company, though out of the work these fifteen years, I hope I have been stung sufficiently to face age without rheumatism.   There are plenty of countrymen who will tell you it is the only sure antidote.

75.—A SUMMER DAY DIARY.

5.0 a.m. (Summer-time)—Go downstairs slowly, not feeling at my best ; there are no excuses for rising at this hour except the heat and the impossibility of sleeping any longer when the swallow that nests in the chimney has flown round the room twice before going out by the window.   Look at some unfinished work on desk and decide promptly not to disturb it so early in the morning. Pigeons in the wood gossip loudly; clearly they are surprised to see me. Walk across meadow; get wet. Dew is a greatly over-rated form of moisture, cunning and insidious. Poets should be compelled to walk through some before they are free to write about it.

5.20 a.m.—Young cuckoo lights on rail fence by the brook. Two foster parents, fly-catchers, are on duty. If they fail to keep cuckoo's large mouth full, cuckoo complains loudly. A dreadful life for fly-catchers. Query: Why have they not evolved a talent for making or at least using fly papers? Pigeons from tree tops jeer at perspiring foster parents.

5.30 a.m.—Mr. and Mrs. Jay and family raid a bean row. Catch a glint of feathers and realise what is going on. Clap my hands. Two parents and four off-spring fly away to the nearest alder and hide in branches, to watch till I move away. Make a note that jays are cunning; this may help students of wild life.

5.50 a.m.—Some hawfinches leave late peas that are being kept for seed and race back to wood. Examine pods and find that field mice have also been attacking them; this taste for peas among the lower orders of creation is to be deplored, but one is pleased to see hawfinches, even though they be bandits.

6.0 a.m.—Gardener busy watering. Left him on the same job at 9.0 p.m. Wonder if he went to bed, but do not ask; he seems active, healthy and well content, and Mother Earth is dry.

6.45 a.m.—Count fifty-eight rabbits in one meadow eating my substance. Vow vengeance. Rabbits continue to eat substance. Pigeons appear to be highly amused; they chuckle coarsely.

7.15 a.m.—See a fish in the brook. Start to dream of trout. Mother cuckoo flies past. She has come round, I think, to see if her baby is being properly cared for by fly-catchers.

7.30 a.m.—Postman arrives and remarks that I am about early. Tell him loftily that I've been working since 5.0 a.m. The touch of imagination pleases me, doesn't hurt him and merely shocks the pigeons. They remark upon the statement but postman can't understand what they say. Letters quite uninspiring.

8.0 a.m.—Ask if breakfast will ever be ready and suggest that it is a pity to waste such a pleasant morning. On receiving explanation, point out that even if the breakfast hour is 8.30, circumstances alter cases.

8.15 a.m.—Breakfast.

8.45 a.m.—Attend to letters.

9.30 a.m.—Daily paper arrives.

9.40 a.m.—Settle down to work.

9.45 a.m.—Telephone bell, wrong number.

9.50 a.m.—Telephone bell, a trivial message.

9.55 a.m.—Telephone bell, Exchange says it did not ring. Say " tut-tut " in a harsh tone.

9.56 a.m.—Home Secretary comes in to ask if I would mind reading certain words that I appear to have written hastily. Find myself unable to oblige. Suggest other words. Express earnest hope that some day she will learn to read my handwriting fluently. She has only to practise. When I studied carefully I could read nearly all of it.

10.0 a.m.—Local Authority says she is running into the town. Do I want anything? Remark coldly that a little of the peace that passeth understanding would be helpful. L.A. says she is sorry and retires. Follow promptly to explain I didn't mean it. She says she knows that. Pigeons greatly surprised. They thought they were the only couples that can coo.

10.15 a.m.—Gardener arrives, panting with indignation. A rabbit has entered vegetable garden and eaten some young lettuce plants, a mole has been running under a flower bed. I offer condolence and commend both intruders to his mercy. He points out that lettuces are scarce just now and adds that they (i.e., rabbits) are varmints. Admit that this may be so.

10.20 a.m. to 12.5 p.m.—Work in the summerhouse. Pigeons above my head talk confidentially, about my industry, I imagine. A gold-crest flits through the larches, a flock of long-tailed tits play havoc with my concentration. A sedge warbler sings in several voices, a friendly attention much appreciated.

12.5 p.m.—Walk steadily. Meet seven farm labourers, four tradesmen, two old ladies in cottage gardens, two tramps, a lad on a bicycle, a school girl and a farmer. All tell me it is a fine day. I knew this. Farmer adds that weather has been good for crops. My only crop, apart from small quantities of fruit and vegetables, being grass that the rabbits have eaten, reply bitterly that he may be right.

1.15 p.m.—Lunch.

1.45 p.m.—Retire to study to read the paper carefully.

2.30 p.m.—Wake with a start.

2.30 p.m. to 4.30 p.m.—Work in study.

4.30 p.m.—Cut down thistles in meadow. Pigeons in larch wood highly amused; they never work.

5.5. p.m.—Gardener very angry indeed, has seen traces of a rat and is about to set four traps in its tracks. Alas, poor offensive rodent.

Drink four cups of tea, only the first two being really required, and the kind I like. But the L.A. says that two are not enough. Husbands, submit yourselves in all things to your Local Authority.

6.0 p.m.—Listen to the news. Gardener has resumed watering with great intensity of purpose. Young cuckoo being fed again. Jays still watching the bean rows from alder tree, to which gardener has driven them. He shouts that if he comes nigh them with a gun . . . Jays ignore threat, knowing he has no gun to hand; pigeons chuckle from the fir tree tops.

6.30 p.m.—Large company of white-throats doing useful work on young fruit bushes, eating aphides. Pigeons sneer vulgarly at them.

7.0 p.m.—Count eighty odd rabbits eating poor remains of my substance in one meadow. Gardener watering. He doesn't mind what happens to my pastures so long as the wire netting protects his vegetables.

7.10 p.m.—Take lurcher down to the meadow where rabbits play. She has a good run. Scores of rabbits pass her by; she ignores them. " Soon as she sees a rabbit, master, she's got it an' she's bringin' it back to ye," said the intelligent countryman from whom I purchased lurcher, rather hastily.

7.30 p.m.—Dinner.

8.15 p.m.—Am unable to number the droves of rabbits steadily reducing meadows to ruin, but am sure that if caught and sold for the benefit of the National Debt, income tax might be reduced. Lurcher rests peacefully in kennel. Gardener watering. He expresses himself vindictively about varmints that enter gardens; ruined meadows and lurchers without enthusiasm leave him cold.

9.0 p.m.—All the land brown with rabbits. They play light-heartedly for joy of having eaten me out of house and home. Gardener watering, pigeons talking about him. He is still bitter about the rabbit, the mole and the rat; and will, I fear, retire in a bad frame of mind. I counsel forgiveness of those that trespass against us.

9.30 p.m.—Moon has risen. A night-jar trills from the bracken by the woodside. There is no other sound in this world just now.

10.0 p.m.—Have read a few chapters and listened to the end of a wireless concert. Jazz music blares from a restaurant. Switch off and go back to garden.

11.0 p.m.—A brown owl cries suddenly that it is time to go to bed. Adds that all bipeds living in or round the wood should leave the night to owls.

11.5 p.m.—Apologise and withdraw.

P.S.—I have not risen again at 5 a.m. But I have advised several young friends to do so.

76.—God's Silver.

Heavy showers had fallen on hot parched fields, the thought of the last mushrooms, so recently " God's silver scattered everywhere," as old folk used to call them when I was a boy, was a clarion call to duty. Unfortunately I forgot for once that the fields would be drenched in dew, but the way down the hill from the cottage is steep and the dew was so instant in its penetration that return seemed out of the question. Dreadfully annoyed, with sodden boots, socks and trouser ends, I quartered the ten-acre meadow and picked a basketful. The two gentlemen who arrived to improve their financial prospects as I was leaving had either failed to rise in time or had taken too long a journey; I searched my make-up

MOWING

for sympathy and could find none. I'm quite sure that their feet were better protected than mine, their boots were probably dressed with mutton fat in the true country fashion.

Mushrooms won from the enemy at the last possible moment have a flavour all their own; when your feet are wet and cold and you have indulged in a preliminary sneeze, charity will not come near you. A few blackberries were sweet and refreshing, I returned to the cottage with my precious burden passing en route the long garden shed, once a super poultry house, where bedded in selected earth and costly stable manure, the expensive mushroom spawn lay so long inactive and inert. I said nothing to the long bed but walked down the side of it, my basket clearly visible to forced specimens had there been any. They had failed to treat us fairly. Wet feet make these failures very bitter.

76.—" ROONS."

"We fall to rise, are baffled to fight better." Robert Browning wrote that and I remember having recited the line to the little block of mushroom spawn, for which I paid four and sixpence. This was our fourth attempt to grow mushrooms in darkness under glass on a bed that had been made with care, tested with the thermometer and worked on at a preliminary cost calculated to make the crop (if any) something in the nature of a luxury. By the side of a mushroom bed call no woman capricious, uncertain, wayward or fickle. This attempt is due to Robert Browning. But for him I would have been content to sow little patches of spawn about the meadows in spring, dress the land with salt and potash and trust to luck. Luck often puts in an appearance in autumn but my trouble is that, having brought the mushrooms, the jade considers her job complete and goes her way.

Certain nondescripts, I know some by sight and by name, steal my crop, not because they want a tasty dish for breakfast, I could forgive that, but because they want the money of certain folk in the nearby town who have a weakness for " roons." Even then if they were philanthropists, if they would say " that man has more than he needs so we have brought you some," I would not complain. But every basket they gather and take to town yields hard cash which they do not even offer to share. I can pay the tithe on the land, dress it with suitable manure, buy spawn, employ labour. The only consolation left to me is that down to the present they have not asked me to pay them for the time they spend picking what they steal. It is not hard to understand why I made this desperate fourth attempt to grow something that no thieving visitors will attack in the early morning hours.

* * * *

He rose high in lonely splendour on his throne in the long house beyond the potting shed. It was not such a throne as all would choose, though it had been prepared by the King's horses fed by the King's men. To be brief and blunt, the throne was of stable manure from the Cavalry barracks, and the ruler who stood solitary on that throne was a mushroom, sole progeny of a " brick " of spawn.

The throne had been erected about midsummer, the spawn built in it, so to speak, and the gardener had spoken hopefully of a waiting period, between six weeks and two months. The weeks sped by. Mushrooms of adequate delicacy followed autumn rain into the fields, diligently the gardener or I gathered what we could before enterprising strangers could raid the meadows ; a friend could write, " My lawn has become a mushroom bed." But in the darkened house where the spawn dwelt in warmth and what, to mushroom spawn is probably comfort, nothing happened.

Then came a frost, a nipping and an eager air, and our breakfast table dish of mushrooms shrank to such narrow dimensions that it could no longer stand alone. Winter in all its bleak disarray stood upon the threshold of our days ; bitterly I said to the gardener, " You had better clear away that bed." At that moment the despised and ruinous heap made its first and last effort, the great mushroom arose in a night, but even then misfortune dogged us. The gardener and I had lost interest, we no longer glanced daily at the barren bed ; the solitary fungus flaunted through his little hour and started to wilt. It was in the moment of its decline that, as folk say in this pleasant country, we " happened of it," a remnant most forlorn of what it was.

To-day the throne has been dismantled and spread in various parts of the garden ; it would not surprise me if in an autumn to come, mushrooms spring up abundantly where it has been dug in. It is a matter for candid confession that so soon as I started to improve the meadow by dressing it with the salts that are said to woo mushrooms irresistibly, the supply fell off. Through two years in succession we did not gather ten pounds, though before I intervened the yield could be measured in bushels. Surely the ways of an eagle in the air or a serpent on a rock or a man with a maid are as nothing in point of mystery compared with the way of mushroom spawn in a bed prepared in strict accordance with the instruction of experts.

CHAPTER XIV

GARDENING

78.—SEASONS.

IN the joy of a sunny hour I spoke of Spring to Mr. Candy, aged cottager who keeps poultry as well as fruit and vegetables.

"Spring," said he a little scornfully, " ain't nothing at all by the good rights. That's just worth a dish o' greens an' a mite o' rhubarb to ye."

"You wake up one morning come April," continued Mr. Candy, "and it's that warm you can't abide it. You wake up next morning and it's a coat colder and the frost bin and got y'r blossoms. You can't trust April ne yet May. Always up to their tricks both of 'em. I know 'em."

"Summer!" remarked Mr. Candy judicially a little later. "Summer's all right, when it does come. I make a fair price o' me red currants an' me rasps and there's folk'll buy lettuces an' early pertaters. I wouldn't mind three Augusts running, time there's folk traipsing about, though hens ain't laying like they should. I speak 'em fair an' I don't ask 'em much money," he added, referring doubtless to traipsing folk.

"It's good to be modest," I said for his encouragement.

"That doesn't do to ast too much nowadays," explained Mr. Candy frankly. "There's too many others in the business. Time I was a boy folk grew what they wanted for themselves. They didn't set any store by strangers, an' if any come along they got to pay or go without. But there, Autumn's best."

"I prefer the Spring."

"You're wrong," said Mr. Candy positively. "Time when folk come along in their moty cars, I've good apples and pears and plums, an' they're Money. When you can sell by the bushel or the peck even, that's Money. And when you've sold all you can, you dig your garden over and tidy up and go set by your fire an' take things easy. You don't look for warm weather ne yet fine days and you take what you get and you're satisfied."

"If you've any eggs by then," he went on, "they're a good price and if you haven't, you've got what you pickled and you can eat them. And you can fat a few birds agen Christmas. You haven't got to go out after weeds, there aren't any more waspses an' there's water in the well."

"I got to work me fingers to the bone come the Spring," concluded Mr. Candy, "and time that's over I'm well rid of it. I never cared for it when I was young; you don't want to keep on in the garden from morning to night."

"Some people will tell you they enjoy gardening for its own sake," I reminded him.

"Let 'em say so," said Mr. Candy loftily. "I ain't no call to believe 'em nor yet ain't you. It's their pocket they're thinking of, an' they might as well be honest about it, same as I am."

79.—WANTED : A GARDENER.

The time had come, happily a long time ago now, to seek another gardener complete with willing wife, for the first lady had wearied of well doing. She had plumped for *otium cum dignitate* and it wasn't to be found here. The gardener was very loyal to his wife; he rebuked us for requiring her services in the house seeing that she felt she had worked long enough. When I pointed out that all the conditions of service had been explained, he pointed out that they had nothing to do with the case; it was not a matter of what we wanted but of what his wife was prepared to give us. Clearly I had been in error. There was time for a careful search and, though temporary arrangements were not too good, I passed from one promise of perfection to another. It was during the period of contemplation that the Hopeful Man called—thick-set, middle-aged, robust, optimistic.

Hopeful Man : " Mornin', guv'nor. They do say you're lookin' for a gardener."

The Scribe : " That is so."

Hopeful Man : " I've come about the job."

The Scribe : " Yes. What is your experience ? "

Hopeful Man : " I've kep' a garden twenty year an' more."

The Scribe : " For whom ? "

Hopeful Man : " For meself, of course."

The Scribe : " Do you understand glass ? Can you raise melons and mushrooms and chrysanthemums ? "

Hopeful Man (scornfully) : " I've never bothered about such things, but I lay I could, if anybody showed me how."

The Scribe : " Then you are not a professional gardener ? "

Hopeful Man (guardedly) : " I'm a gardener right enough."

The Scribe : " Married ? "

Hopeful Man : " Lord love ye, nigh thirty year."

The Scribe : " Any children ? "

Hopeful Man : " Three little 'uns but they don't give no trouble. The others are all at work."

The Scribe : " I'm afraid I don't want children. My advertisement said so quite plainly."

Hopeful Man : " Your piece in the paper, you mean. I didn't take any count o' that bit."

The Scribe : " A pity. I'm afraid you're not the man I'm looking for. What are you by trade ? "

Hopeful Man : " A gardener I tell ye. Thanks. (Lights

proffered cigarette.) If you want a plain gardener I'm the man for you."

The Scribe (persuasively and taking a long shot): "But when you're not on your allotment, what do you do?"

Hopeful Man (frankly, recognising a hopeless case when he sees one): "Well, guv'nor, if you really want to know, I'm a plumber. But business ain't none too good jes' now, an' I see your piece in the paper an' Maria, that's my wife, said 'Go and try, George. You never know.' So as I was cyclin' out this way, I thought I'd call. If you didn't want a lot o' fancy things, I could keep your garden a treat."

The Scribe: "I'm afraid I do want just a few specials, and I must have a gardener whose wife will help in the house."

Hopeful Man: "Me Maria wouldn't do that. There's the three little 'uns an' two come in from work an' want their hot supper." (Reproachfully) "You don't want to ask a woman to neglect her own flesh and blood." (Regretfully) "But there I could ha' kept the garden all right." (Resignedly) "Well, I ain't wasted much time. That's a comfort, I had to come far as th' Mill. Good mornin'."

80.—GARDEN LORE.

The L.A., who is at once the companion of my way, chatelaine of the cottage and final arbiter on all matters relating to a garden, has a "growing hand." Do you know the term? It is applied to people in whose footsteps the flowers rise and flourish.

With you and me, certainly with me, planting is a hit or miss affair, with them the element of uncertainty is negligible. A garden is their first medium of self-expression whatever else their gifts, because love of flowers is part of their life; they know almost intuitively the best position, the most suitable soil, the right depth, the proper moment. They can see a bank of colour before it is in being, planning a bed in Autumn, they know what the Spring effect will be. · When Spring comes they can plant in fashion that will carry the season of colour and bloom to the hour when black frost or heavy snow cannot be withstood.

A GARDEN PATH

I don't think you can teach anybody to acquire a " growing hand." It is as much a response to unseen forces as water-finding.

When you seek to create a garden out of a weed-patch, a period of doubt and dissatisfaction is inevitable. But so soon as the first section, however small, shows healthy flowers above clean, fragrant soil, you hear the opening chords of the great symphony that will develop its many themes for you without a pause until the time comes when you pass out of hearing of all the songs of Mother Earth. There will be the *allegro* of Spring, the *scherzo* of Summer, the *andante* of Autumn, but the fourth great movement will not have any finale, it will merge in the *allegro* again when another year is born. A very pleasant sense of elation comes with the possession of a garden ; you have a share of the world's most exquisite gift and since we cannot be happy as sole possessors of anything we must needs share our garden with all true garden lovers. They are rare. Time was when I would take people I cared for round the garden to enjoy their reactions. Time is when I know that these reactions may not be forthcoming and I have long ceased to run personally-conducted tours. But sometimes the L.A. and I walk in the garden in the cool of the evening and remember the birth of the world.

Suffering from a bright idea I took certain steps on behalf of those who buy collections of vegetable seeds, thinking that my efforts might provide some valuable comparisons. Seeds were purchased from four different firms. They were to be kept apart and numbered and their achievement recorded. The first came from a renowned house and expensive, the second came from an enterprising rival firm that does not look upon the value of its produce with quite such a dilated eye, the third from a commercial house to which many seedsmen turn, and the fourth from a firm that sells in sixpenny, threepenny, and even twopenny packets, and bids you be of good faith and high hope. All the seeds were sown on similar soil and carefully tended. But after the first year when I made enquiry, with every intention of making some very helpful notes, all had been mixed. There was nothing to be said, for I had not taken the trouble to see that my instructions were being carried out, and the gardener was even busier than I. Moreover, as I buy the seeds he asks for, he had no special interest in my experiment.

I follow certain of the theories of juxtaposition of plants advocated by the followers of Dr. Rudolph Steiner. They sow nasturtiums by their apple trees, horseradish by their potatoes, limiting its range by trenching and filling the trench with manure from pigsties ; they plant their strawberries for choice near pine trees. I have placed nasturtiums round some apple trees, horseradish near one potato patch and I have planted a few strawberries close to the pines. Others grown in the ordinary way, without their alleged aids, serve as what are called " controls." In the first three years of my endeavour the frosts intervened twice.

There is another theory taught by Dr. Steiner's followers and proved, I think, beyond doubt. They say that vegetables fruiting above the ground should be sown when the moon is rising ; then they have far earlier growth than those sown under a waning moon. I am testing the theory. There are upwards of a thousand market gardens on the Continent where the Steiner methods used to be followed, just a handful in England. But this method is a part of the countryman's lore and was practised in the heart of our countryside centuries before Dr. Steiner lived.

Mr. Tripp provided a confirmation that was not unexpected, because he belongs to the old school that inherited traditions and has never despised them, all his contempt being reserved for the generation following his own.

"Did you plant those peas on a rising moon ? " I asked.

"Nobody but a fool," declared Mr. Tripp roundly, "would goo a sowin' top-ground wegables time th' moon's shrinkin'. That wouldn't be no sense."

"Who taught you that ? " I asked him.

"Me father larnt me," admitted the old man, conquering a certain reluctance, "an' his father larnt him. Time th' moon's comin' is allus better than when she's a gooin'. If I was to kill me pig time th' moon lay on her back," he added solemnly, pointing to the sty, "she'd be mostly bound to waste."

I ventured to take it for granted that it was the pig and not the moon that would waste, or at least that the pig would waste in sympathy with the moon. Every old Suffolk farm labourer would accept this view. Dr. Steiner gave authority to beliefs that must have passed down through the centuries, beliefs jealously preserved by Mr. Tripp and his fellow-gardeners in a thousand villages in these islands. Truly there is nothing new under the sun ; we forget and we remember, and when we remember we think we have made a discovery. The moon and stars have a place in our lives long forgotten, much derided, but sure to be recognised before the world is much older.

In the cultivation of garden and orchard too many poisons are employed. Seeds are protected from insects by the aid of mercury ; we spray our trees with arsenate of lead and copper sulphate, we clean garden paths with arsenic. There is a steadily growing school of thinkers and students that holds these methods dangerous. Scientific investigation has traced all manner of harmful chemicals from wheat grain to loaf, from vine to wine-glass, from fruit tree to dessert dish. People who have studied the subject tell us that we owe most of the diseases of our orchard and vegetable garden to over-stimulation of the soil, to our endeavours to speed up natural rates of growth ; some will declare that we are robbing the land of its humus and that the mixture of mineral with vegetable is an unholy alliance. They say that our poisoned food accounts for a great part of the complaints from which we suffer. We are what we eat. Since the advent of mineral fertilisers, foot-and-mouth disease and fluke in sheep, wart and canker in vegetables, to say nothing of insect pests, have multiplied and the deaths from cancer per million have risen from less than two hundred to nearly sixteen hundred. There is surely a case for enquiry.

Here our fruit and vegetables have no contact with mineral stimulants, they are not sprayed with mineral mixtures. Vegetable composts and a few simple preparations of plant life replace the usual dressings. Experts tell me that in addition to getting absolutely healthy food, we shall find a better quality. This remains to be proved ; it is sufficient to fly in the face of custom and practise methods which, if successful, should prove of real value to thousands who have never heard of them.

I am surrounded by fruit farms, now thriving if the weather permits, where the annual cost of sprays, washes, hand-machines and labour must be considerable. It is common knowledge that where chemical mixtures are used on fruit trees, without a large measure of due care, foraging bees die, in any event moles and earthworms disappear. Yet fertilisation of fruit trees by bees is of admitted importance ; worm and mole have their appointed tasks, and the health of the fruit on many farms round me is only pre-served by the aid of poison. I have said as much and am very properly unpopular, just as an assertive ignoramus should be.

While we are looking forward to still better results and experiencing the keen delight of Springtide gardening, the local Jeremiahs continue to practise lamentations.

" You on't grow much there, Master," one of them assured me ; " telly f'r why. That's all sand an' gravel you got there."

" Have you ever been over it ? " I enquired.

" I ain't exactly been over it," he admitted, " but there's a many what has."

" We've had some splendid crops," I assured him.

" You don't wanter talk so," he replied reproachfully, " being I was born here, an' you on'y come inter these parts yesterday like."

81.—JERRY.

There are times when we cannot keep pace with garden work. Weeds seem to think they should seed at least as freely as flowers and vegetables and that none should wish to dispossess them of land over which they have ruled for years. They are quite undisciplined, the stern brutality of the hoe, the searching inquisitions of fork or spade are called for. If at the time when the work is behind hand, and the gardener has his hands full, the desk is also insistent, there is no help other than first aid. This was why I visited Mr. Jeremiah Nitt—Jerry to his intimates—that old, tried countryman whose brother worked for me long years ago. Mr. Nitt, now enjoying a pension, devotes the late afternoon of his days to a garden which is in perfect order and full in due season of such country flowers as stocks, fuchsias, London pride, honesty, bergamot, thrift, candytuft, sweet william. I found him in his summer-house, smoking his pipe and surveying the herbaceous border with complete content.

" Jerry," I began, when we had passed the time of day, " would you come across to the other side and take two or three weeks in the garden, if I put you up ? Your sister wouldn't mind, perhaps ? "

Mr. Nitt pondered deeply.

" That'd be very hazardable," he said ; " I doubt I dussn't."

" What's the difficulty ? " I enquired.

" That's along o' me pension," he whispered.

" Mr. —— wouldn't mind," I assured him, naming the benevolent employer to whom he owes latter-day ease.

" That ain't him," whispered Mr. Nitt. " That's Govinment."

" What has Government to do with it ? " I queried.

" Soon as ever they find ye doin' a job o' work, they go to stop y'r money," he said, still *sotto voce*. " I know 'em, the mucks. Artful as monkeys is Govinment; allus got a eye on ye."

" Yours isn't a Government pension," I explained. " They can't touch it."

" Ah," replied Mr. Nitt, still speaking in tones too low for Government to hear, " I count you're wrong. They'll touch anybody's money, th' varmints, soon as look at it. That's all they care about, to rob ye. I bin an' read a piece in the paper about it. If I took a job f'r anybody, they'd know it next day. Double cunnin', that's what they are. If they think you got a shillin' in y'r pocket, they're out arter it d'reckly minit."

You may say that Mr. Nitt was wrong. I did the same, but he remained quite unmoved. " Me son got a friend what got a pension, an' he took a job an' got hisself in th' wrong, right away. Th' magistret should ha' said a man gotter give up his money time he got a job, an' towd him to goo to prison. Jeremiah Nitt ain't a gooin' to prison his time o' life, t'ain't likely." So saying, Mr. Nitt relit his pipe by way of terminating discussion.

82.—LIKELY LAD.

When my appeal for extra help had been refused by the old-time helper who mistrusts the Government and fears for his pension, I made further enquiry, and was directed to a " likely lad." He, too, lives a long way off, but there is accommodation here. I found him standing by the gate of his parents' charming cottage-garden, hands in pocket, his father does the gardening. We chatted.

The Scribe : " I hear you're out of a job. Are two or three weeks any use to you ? "

Likely Lad (cautiously) : " What's the work ? "

The Scribe : " Gardening and rough carpentry. It might last longer, if we suit one another."

WHERE GARDEN MERGES INTO WOODS

Likely Lad : " Thanks, but I don't want to stop about here. I want to get out of the country."

The Scribe : " Why ? "

Likely Lad : " I've an uncle down New Cross way. I'm gooin' to run arrands and learn me way about, then I'll find something. That's better than farmin'. Good money in a little while, too, if you have any luck."

The Scribe : " You don't like country life ? "

Likely Lad : " No, I don't. Father's bin at it all his life an' gets tharty-two shillin's a week." (This, of course, was before the war.)

The Scribe : " But this cottage can't cost him more than three shillings and your garden's full of fruit and vegetables, and I see you've a wireless."

Likely Lad : " At New Cross they got pichers across the road an' forever o' public housen, an' buses, an' newspapers, an' heaps o' folk to talk to. That's what I'm looking for."

The Scribe : " Good luck to you."

Likely Lad : " Thanky."

CHAPTER XV

AN ENEMY

83.—A Thief of the Night.

He crept out of his hole in the bank beyond the woodside gate when night was young and the moon full; he moved with extreme caution among the shadows, his colour blending with his surroundings so that he had but to crouch in order to become invisible.

Broad shining spaces frightened him; when he came to one that must be crossed, he ran, his tail leaving a mark on the ground. He could no longer keep it lifted, for old age was upon him. Somebody had shut the gate and filled the gap between post and frame, but he scrambled up the wire to where a broken mesh enabled him to slip through. There he paused.

A cluster of wych elm saplings offered shelter; slinking towards it he waited, listening and alert. Suddenly barn owl called from the woodside; he lay almost level with the ground while the bird swept across the glade and down the meadow, passing within ten yards. Had he moved, had

she glimpsed him, she would have dropped; her claws
would have closed on his heart. Now she was among the
alders skimming past outer branches on the look out for
little birds that roost foolishly. Her note, so expressive
of anger, hunger and anxiety, was soon subdued by distance;
he moved securely out of cover to the side of the big outhouse.
But he did not seek his goal directly, that would be contrary
to all hereditary instinct; there were two big rolls of wire
netting left to be set up, with just enough space between
for him to squeeze through. By the side was a bench;
the gardener sits on it sometimes to eat bread and cheese
round about eleven o'clock; he drops a few crumbs; they
are sweet. Now only a small piece of bread was left; he
ate it greedily. Then he crept up to the house, seeking the
hole he had made two nights earlier, stopped, sniffed and
turned away. Traps; he could see the outline of one;
by the gift that he retains and man has lost he recognised the
taint of a human hand that had set another. Those traps
guarded a bag of beans he had opened and rifled only
twenty-four hours earlier; he must find another way to food.
He had not roamed those outbuildings for three years without
acquiring knowledge; he could sense danger with uncanny
prescience; his age was tribute to his cunning; he had
few contemporaries.

Now he was through another wire gate, left open this time,
and by the side of the first range of lights next the conservatory. He sniffed the soil carefully. Here, at least, the
ground had not been tampered with; he set to work and
scraped a hole beneath. Sandy soil flew behind him in
a tiny cloud; he stopped only to listen and in fifteen minutes
was in the melon frame, with its opening into the conservatory,
where late tomatoes were ripening. He crept through and
pulled one piece of fruit from a low-lying truss and ate
eagerly, for he felt thirsty, but such food was not to his
liking. He liked to change his diet, to pass from flesh to
vegetable and grain, and then again to flesh—any carrion
would serve. Soon he turned to go, but could not find the
way because he had gone back into the wrong light, or at least
it was not the one he had entered; there was no place of
exit, and he must scrape, scrape hard and anxiously. The

night was hot, his thirst terrible, the tomato had not quenched it ; he dared not go back because he was afraid, even though he knew not why. But he had found a place where the soil was soft ; he tore uncleared bine from side to side to make a path, careless that he was writing a record that any trained eye could read, and in a little while was free, free to return to wood, shadow, and rill.

Then he remembered another entrance ; one he had made recently and forgotten. It was intact and untainted ; he ran through into the place where bags of seed could be had for the asking. But no; there had been a change; the bags had been gathered, they stood on the shelves of a safe made of galvanised fine-mesh wire netting with stout metal frame. Only the beans remained with their cruel guard. The hole he deemed unknown had been left for his destruction. Invisible to his enemies they were invisible to him, but the struggle between him and man was unending ; cunning pitted against cunning. Now he slunk back and sought the open, baffled, tired, dispirited. It was an effort to climb the wire, but at last the bank was before him.

Suddenly he rushed forward blindly, only just in time. He had heard the swift descent above him, almost felt the noise of the resistance of the air as spread wings broke the pace, and he escaped by inches from the owl that had swooped from the ash tree. But as he lay supine there was no further impulse to stir, just a thirst, an overwhelming thirst that he dared not move to quench, lest the white owl should be biding her time. A few moments later he knew that if there were never an owl in the wood and a stream were at his feet he could not rise to drink. His limbs stiffened and his eyes glazed, while the light breaking in the east dimmed the long-drawn-out pageant of the Hunter's moon. Death had come to him, he knew not whence nor how.

*　　　*　　　*

"He was here again last night," said the gardener, a few hours later, "but he wouldn't look at the traps ; knew all about them ; he must have been a very old rat ; he went in and out as if he didn't know quite what he did want. I've tried to get him time and again and he's been too clever for me, but now I've done the trick. He took the little bit

of bread and butter I slipped down between the wire. I've
fed a few crumbs there these three days past where birds
couldn't touch them and he's been clearing them up. We
shan't see him again. I've never tried this poison before;
it was new to him; if he'd met it before he wouldn't have
looked at it."

84.—CRUELTY.

The small boy opened the gate gingerly, eyed the L.A.,
Nelly, and Tich with anxiety, gathered courage on being
assured that the dogs had already had their supper, and
came up to us with a collecting box held before him, as though
to explain and qualify intrusion.

"If you please," he said, "will you help Cruelty to
Animals?"

"There's something in that," I said to the L.A., for Nelly
the lurcher and Tich the kennel terrier had been running
over flower beds, and though she loves flowers, the L.A.
is apt to find excuses for both. "What animals are you
cruel to?" I enquired, and the boy seemed puzzled.

"It's dogs, I think, in X," he replied, naming the nearest
town.

"Nothing could be better," I said cheerily. "And are
people subscribing well to cruelty?"

"Yessir," he said proudly. "I got eleven and six already."

The L.A. and I were without money, but her purse was in
the porch, and while she sought it I went to the gate, where
another small boy stood waiting for his companion in
enterprise to return. He held one bicycle and guarded
another; perhaps they rode hastily from bad receptions.

"Are you helping cruelty to animals?" I enquired.

"Yessir," he told me proudly, and I realised that they
also serve who only stand and wait!

"What do you get out of all your hard work?" I enquired
of the first comer, when he came back from the porch.

"I shan't know, sir, until I get back," he replied guardedly.

The box had a label, and from it I gathered, without
surprise, that the purpose of the appeal was not cruelty to
animals but its prevention, the young collectors, being
without prejudice, were satisfied to collect, and their

employers, being doubtless highly intelligent, were equally content to receive the collection.

85.—THE RIGHT OF THE ROAD.

The hiking season has come round again. Questions of trespass loom large. There are two sides to them. The first and most important is the right of a public, driven from roads by reckless motorists or even by its own heedlessness, to enjoy the lovely countryside that fringes the formal ways of rural England. The second is the right of the landowner to preserve his property.

All infringements of reasonable private rights are the work of a careless or thoughtless minority. For the past thirty years I have owned land that has offered summer attraction to hikers. A few have sought, others have taken permission to use it. I have asked those I have met to light no fires and leave no rubbish. There has been a certain friendliness on both sides. As one who eats in the open air in fine weather, and nearly always on other people's land, I follow the rule of burying or carrying away all litter.

So far as the law of trespass is concerned, there is much lack of understanding. Many landowners disfigure the country with lying notices to the effect that trespassers will be prosecuted. They will not. If you and I walk over another man's land, breaking no barrier or hedge and doing no damage, the worst that can happen to us is a request by owner or his representative to return to the public way. If we refuse, necessary force may be used to turn us out, but if on learning that our presence is an intrusion, we leave at once, there is no action he can take. Trespassers are not prosecuted for trespass, only for damage. In Scotland when I was much younger I put up a notice about trespass in an endeavour to keep hikers from walking over a grouse moor and disturbing my birds ; people laughed and told me that in Scotland they knew nothing about trespass. It was easier to take down the notice than to live down the memory of a silly blunder.

There are innumerable rights-of-way that have been closed arbitrarily throughout England and Wales, but happily there is a Commons and Footpaths Preservation Society, the terror of men eager to curtail the public right ; it helps to free the land for the enjoyment of one and all.

I should like to see every company of men and women or boys and girls that practises hiking accept certain rules of conduct and appoint some of the party to guard their observance. One might be responsible for closing gates ; if they are left open, stock may stray and the farmer suffer damage. Another should see that, where necessary, walking in single file shall be the rule, a third might be responsible to see that no live cigarette ends are thrown down and no fires are lighted in any place where it is possible for grass or hedge to be scorched, and that, before the party leaves, all fire is dead. It would be better still if fires were ruled out altogether. Another excellent rule would be that no flowers should be picked to be thrown away and that none should be taken up by the roots. Finally, the disposal of all litter by burial would complete the list of rules that every hiking company might well impose upon itself. They are simple enough but if adopted by parties large and small, and carried out scrupulously, the outcries of indignant landowners would be stilled and disastrous heath or forest fires unknown. These little rules of conduct would do nothing to check the enjoyment of a holiday, indeed sensitive people would be pleased to think that nobody could reasonably regard their ramble on other folk's land as matter for grievance. During a dry spell I walked in the wood among the larches with a man who had been telling me of a bad forest fire in Surrey. He is an ardent smoker and I trod on the ends of three cigarettes he had thrown away before he realised what he had been doing.

The countryman is often in worse plight than the hiker. His area is limited, he can't go from one county to another at will, he must stay put, his range is limited not by his own capacity to walk, which may be excellent, but by that of his wife and children whom he cannot leave behind when Sunday comes. He knows all the field paths, they have been familiar to him since childhood, but they are hard to maintain. He has seen the plough pass over them and the arable crop or the orchard obliterate the track ; he has felt that he must not complain, since if he does he may be up against his own employer, and there is little room on the land even to-day for sturdy men who lack proper respect for authority. He hasn't heard of the Commons and Footpaths Preservation Society and would hesitate to invoke its aid if he did ; he cannot afford to seek trouble.

In our own backward parish I remember urging a man who complained that a very pleasant path had been unlawfully closed to appeal to the Council. He was asking me how to do so when his wife intervened. " John don't want to do that," she said uneasily, " he can't." Thereupon I advised the man not to proceed because I could see that there would be trouble for him if he did, his wife was so obviously distressed. The reason was explained by a neighbour who knew that countryside better than I did.

" If he were to make trouble about that footpath she might lose that job as occasional cook at ' the house,' and it means quite a lot to her with only her husband's small wage and a young family to look after."

The hikers who, giving no ground for criticism, open up the byways and enjoy England, are not only helping themselves. They help obscure countrymen who cannot voice their rights. Their activities might be multiplied to the public advantage.

86.—EASILY SHOCKED.

" If you weren't a married man along of your wife," said old Mrs. Tibbits, indicating the Local Authority who was picking harebells from the hedgerow, " I dussn't hardly talk about 'em, an' that's th' truth, sure as I set here."

The old lady pointed across her garden to the straggling fruit trees of the nearby farmer's orchard. A small white tent stood up modestly, two slim figures were at work nearby.

" One of 'em's a man," continued Mrs. Tibbits, " but th' other ain't. I'm mos'ly ashamed to say it."

" A young married couple," I suggested. " It's very good to be young."

" She was wearing a wedding ring right enough," admitted Mrs. Tibbits cautiously, " but I ain't see her lines. An' if she's as married as I am, that's no excuse for goin' about so.

If you'd asked me which was the girl and which was the boy, I'd have bin wholly puzzled until I heard 'em talkin'.''

"Hikers," I explained, "go all over the country nowadays. Hiking makes a happy, healthy holiday enough."

"But a girl don't want to wear breeches, beggin' your pardon for namin' 'em," protested Mrs. Tibbits. "If I'd gone out in sech things me mother would have given me sech a box on the ear that th' wall would 'na' give me another. She'd liefer have seen me in me cawfin," continued Mrs. Tibbits passionately.

"Where would you have chosen to be?" I enquired. "In the coffin alone, or in the orchard with your husband and a tent and some sort of a stove so far as I can see, to cook a meal on? After all your mother wouldn't have called for her own coffin because you dressed like a boy, and she would have had no right to call for yours!"

"Nobody wants to die afore their time," admitted Mrs. Tibbits more mildly, "and that's only a manner o' speaking to say she'd have wanted me dead an' gone, but that don't prevent a woman putting on a skirt, does it now? After all, a girl's a girl and a boy's a boy, and if boys don't wear skirts girls don't want to wear trousers."

"But they do want to, evidently," I persisted.

"Then they oughter be ashamed o' theirselves," cried Mrs. Tibbitts, becoming hard once more, and turning her garden chair round sufficiently to avoid further offence to her eyes.

87.—HIKERS.

A little company of hikers tramped down the lane and passed civil greeting. Mr. Tripp, apparently too annoyed to acknowledge it, allowed me to respond for both.

"I've no use for sech," he growled. "Always traipsing about. Here this week an' somewhere else the week after. Can't stop still, I doubt."

"What harm do they do?" I enquired.

"Forever of harm," said Mr. Tripp. "Cap'en Tottle come past mine one day last week an' told me he should have found ten of 'em in one of his meadows, eatin' their vittles, bold as brass."

THE ROAD BY THE WOOD

"Had they done any damage or left any litter?" I enquired.

"He said they'd shut th' gate all right an' clent up arter them that time," explained Mr. Tripp a little reluctantly, "but they're bound to tell another lot, an' some of 'em will leave the gates an' chuck paper all over the place. Don't tell me. They do it on my wireless reg'lar, an' somebody scold 'em for it. But, bless you, they don't care."

"Cap'en Tottle should say," continued Mr. Tripp confidently, "that there's a sight too many foot paths everywheres. 'Nowadays,' he says, 'there ain't the call for 'em. Every boy an' every girl got a bicycle and th' roads are better that ever. They can ride fifty mile if they want to,' he says, 'an' not get so much as a puncher, but stiddy that, they come walkin' over me land. Foot paths aren't for sech,' he sez. 'The man who owns the fields ought to own the foot paths,' he sez, 'an' then we shouldn't have all this trouble.' He knows what's what. He won't have folk walkin' over his property if he kin keep 'em out. Puts up barbed wire in the Spring an' takes it down in the Autumn, time cubbin' begins. You gotter allow that's genteel thing to do."

I was purposely incoherent, for the man who closes rights of way and endeavours to bluff his poor neighbours into a belief that his privilege is beyond question or dispute is not to my liking. I know several of them and find them the least desirable of fellow citizens, even while recognising that their anti-social attitude is probably founded on an inferiority complex. If I'm not mistaken the frog in Aesop's fable that tried to swell to the size of the bull suffered from the same devastating complaint, and would have closed paths to his pond or his meadows had he been able to do so in order to keep other frogs out, and let them know what a fine fellow he was.

" Do you know," he continued, lowering his voice, " what some o' them hikers done to him las' year ? " I signified ignorance.

" You ouldn't believe," he went on, " but there, nobody wouldn't. He'd put up six strand o' barbed wire front of a field an' the mucks cut it through. One of 'em," said Mr. Tripp wisely, " must have had clippers. He couldn't ha' done it without he had. The Cap'en was reg'lar upset ; he bin to the p'liceman an' towd him all about it. What do you think o' that ? "

I felt too overcome by the thought of so much depravity to seek for adequate expression.

88.—" TRAIPSING."

Some time later Mr. Tripp sat in his porch where the wind and weather could not reach him ; he hailed me and beckoned to the other and less sheltered seat—an unexpected compliment.

" I ain't seen you hereabouts," he began.

" It has been rather a busy time with us," I explained. " We went away, too, for a little while."

" Nobody dedn't ast ye to stop, seemingly," said Mr. Tripp a little sourly, " being you're back agen." He does not approve of change.

" You're quite right," I admitted.

" Stands to reason," he went on. " Folk don't want people comin' interferin', an' astin' a lot o' questions. They want to be left alone."

"There are plenty of men, and women, too, ready to talk about their work," I persisted.

"Lazy mucks, I call sech," cried Mr. Tripp indignantly. "If they done their jobs same as they oughter, they wouldn't be able to stop and chatter.   When I'm in my garden I don't wanter talk to folk—leastaways, not for long," he added, remembering perhaps that he never fails to hail me when I pass down the lane.

"Look at that," he added, pointing to the ordered array of flower and vegetable ground.   "Yours ain't looking like that, I lay."

"I don't think we are quite so neat," I admitted.

"Not be half," he retorted.   "That ought to be a lesson to ye, not to go traipsing about.   If the Good Lord wanted folk to go about everywhere, they'd ha' had wings same as birds."

"Did you never go on a journey?" I asked him.

"I went to the seaside once in a sharrybang," Mr. Tripp admitted, "but I've been sorry ever since.   Next morning after I come back an' looked round me garden, I found somebody bin in an' stripped me red currants.   Four bushes, mind ye, an' red currants makin' fippence a pound.   That was a lesson to me.   If a man got a garden worth lookin' at, he can't go here, there an' everywhere, t'ain't likely.   I oughter towd th' policeman to look arter it for me time I bin away.

"But there," he went on, "you don't wanter be tetchy. I got a few apples I shan't need ; good keepers, mind ye, an' I bin savin' 'em against you come along.   You kin have 'em four shillings a bushel.   There's a many'd ask five. I remembered 'em soon as I see ye."

"That's why you asked me in?" I suggested.

"Surely," replied Mr. Tripp candidly.   "I've no time f'r talkin' about nothin'.   I ain't like some folk what don't work f'r a livin'.   I'll get one o' them apples for you to have a look at.   Then you kin fetch 'em.   I'll be glad to be riddy o' them.   I ain't forever o' store room."

CHAPTER XVI

AUTUMN

89.—Autumn Harvest.

WHEN the late Summer and early Autumn meet, Nature's harvest is well worth gathering. Round us here it includes hazel nuts, elderberries (for wines, cordial or jelly), dewberries, blackberries, and rowans (jelly all the time, please), mushrooms of several kinds, a few wild strawberries, raspberries, and crab apples. We dry the surplus mushrooms and, given a good season, they will last through the year.

Where the nuts are concerned, I insist that the squirrels share them with me, but that is not unreasonable, for when the food scraps from the house are fed to the chickens in the wood the squirrels are uninvited guests. Elderberries belong in a sense to the birds, but as we feed birds all through the winter and elderberry jelly is a pleasant sweet, it is reasonable that we should have some. Rowans (mountain-ash fruits) make a sharp, tasty conserve. Nature is bountiful with blackberries, and all interested parties can come on in that act and take a part. The wild strawberries and raspberries need sharp eyes for a small harvest, crap apples often go neglected for only the country folk know where to look for them and few have the time to turn them into jelly. They should not be picked until they have faced a frost or two.

There are many other wayside gifts that the old country folk know, blackthorn leaves in place of tea for example, and there is an agreeable little root called the pignut that may be found in summer fields by the discerning.

At the time I wrote these notes the hazel by the cover's edge was showing nuts in plenty, hawthorn was full of berries, some trees in the wood across the valley showed a delicate tinge as of burnt umbre.

" There has been a touch of frost ; we'll have no more marrows." The gardener was speaking ; he had supplied a concrete instance to set my abstractions in proper form.

" You're right," I told him ; " summer is over."

I would not work after breakfast ; I walked instead.

There was no sign of mist but there were many signs of "mellow fruitfulness." Pear and apple trees heavy laden, the orange and scarlet and gold of virginia, ampelopsis and other creepers blazed, there was a hop that had climbed over the south wall of a cottage and covered it with lemon-coloured fruit. Some folk were clearing their gardens and burning rubbish, smoke was mounting steeply, untouched by wind. A threshing machine droned in a farmyard. I stayed to watch golden sheaves tossed on to the drum. Ploughs were out breaking the bright stubbles, honest plough teams with two or even three horses are more soothing to the eye than the merciless, efficient tractor. A gaffer sat in the ivied porch of a cottage, sunning himself; we passed the time of day.

"That's bin a rare summer, to my thinkin'," he said. "I can't mind many like it and me in me seventy seven and keep me own garden an' all." It was small, neat and cared for, two beds on either side, a gravel path from the gate to where he sat, beyond the beds some fruit trees in full bearing. "Pick what ye like," urged the veteran. "Tuppence a pound off the trees an' a penny windfalls."

"A great harvest," I said.

"That'll keep me in baccy most all th' winter, thanks be to th' dear Lord," he replied piously, "an' me scales is in th' kitchen. You kin weigh them f'r y'rself." Large Bramley seedlings, sound Pitmastons, but the resources of the cottage did not include a bag and until you have tried to follow instructions and "wrop" them, without the aid of string, in the pages of a popular but unpleasant Sunday paper, a paper that seldom holds anything so clean and healthy as fruit, you cannot understand how difficult it is. Happily good fortune sent the grocer's cart down the lane and the grocer had a brown paper bag.

90.—THE SAINTS OF AUTUMN.

Only the first moods of Autumn are kind, though she must remember and respect both St. Luke and St. Martin, for each brings his own little Summer. It is easy for her to hold out a hand to the Evangelist, but I think she finds it difficult to extend to St. Martin a charity equal to his own. And yet, until he has enjoyed his brief season she may not turn towards her old lover, Winter, and allow him to strip the last of her beauties. Autumn is a lady of many moods, influenced by the Summer when she is young and by Winter in her season of maturity. She is our ever lessening barrier against cold and wind and bitter air, the brief days, the nights when the countryside is so desolate and so bare that even a full moon cannot redeem it. When March sun shines you can be a prodigal; you are about to enter into your kingdom. But when November is within hail, you must treasure every sunny hour, see that each of its sixty minutes is savoured, see that you are gratefully and happily mindful of the day in which it played a part.

91.—Fruit.

I had been taking a friend home, and a short cut brought us past Mr. Tripp's cottage. He held up his hand to stop us. "Of all men else, I have avoided thee," I quoted.

"You don't wanter avoid folk," retorted Mr. Tripp reproachfully. "I might ha' let ye goo on and took no notice, but I never. I sez, time I see ye comin', I gotter tell him about his white currants what I promised him."

"I remember," I replied, without enthusiasm; he had been lavish in promises; the currants were to be payment for seeds supplied.

"You couldn't be off o' rememberin'," said Mr. Tripp sharply, "being I grow the best hereabouts. But there," he added, "that ain't what ye grow, that's what happen to it. Couldn't stand the sun they couldn't, pore things. That took 'em, time they was too tender. You just shook th' owd bush and they fell down. That was the same," he continued, "along o' me strawberries. They came along lookin' a treat, an' then th' sun come and took advantage of 'em. You won't wanter talk to me o' fruit," said Mr. Tripp severely, "an' that ain't no use you lookin' to me for any."

"I hadn't any idea of doing so," I retorted, not perhaps so affably as I should have done.

"That's where you're wrong," he replied. "Come most

years me fruit's a masterpiece. But you can't go agen Nature. Folk what go agen Nature jest get theirselves muddled up. I promised ye white currants an' I've kep' me word; I've told ye why ye can't have none. If you bin th' King of England," concluded Mr. Tripp severely, " an' I hadn't got no white currants, I couldn't give ye none."

Since our brief encounter, I learn on good authority that I visited Mr. Tripp and " carried on wunnerful " because he hadn't any white currants, showing no sympathy with him on the loss of his soft fruit, through the coming of a dry spell at the end of May and in the beginning of June. Happily Mr. Tripp stood up to me and refused to be browbeaten by somebody who does not even " belong round here." It is well to remember that in the country you are at the mercy of the most casual happenings. They establish your reputation, very unfavourably as a rule.

Then again, Mr. Tripp may have been content with a few words of well-merited condemnation of one whom he suspected of wanting white currants and when his comment had passed from mouth to mouth, gathering momentum so to speak all the time, it must needs become a formidable indictment when it reached me.

Your countryman combines a harsh tongue with a kind heart, so it is never well to take rough words too seriously. He is emphatic lest his comment should be overlooked and this little failing is not limited to those who live in the rural areas.

92.—A NIGHT OUT.

THE Hunter's moon has risen from where the rainbow ends and is wearing a veil of gossamer, woven in cloudland. The valley below us, through which Black Brook runs so gaily to the distant river, is calling to life a long, vaporous figure corresponding roughly to the length and direction of the stream. It might be the spirit of the water, made manifest by night's decree; it is merely such a mist as rises from water meadows in Autumn.

Across the valley the wood meets the horizon; a mass of oak trees whose foliage, still undimmed, is cut in silhouette against the sky. Overhead, invisible, a late-flying aeroplane

NIGHTJARS.

drones away through space to fade into distance and leave silence in unchallenged possession of Mother Earth. And as though pleased with the mood of the hour, the moon strips her veils and stands out in unabashed splendour.

"It seems a shame to sleep through such a night," says the L.A., standing by my side in the porch; it is bedtime, and the day, like all our days, has been well filled with little tasks that call for attention rather than effort, tire pleasantly and leave no trace.

"Let us see it through," I suggest. "Put a kettle on the top of the water heater and we can take a couple of rugs and a torch to the summer-house."

" Really ? " asks the L.A.

" It will be jolly," I assure her and her interest wakes.

" I'll see to the things," she whispers ; we have been talking *sotto voce* all the time ; there are hours that subdue the voice.

11.30.   The silence is profound.   Moonlight has flooded one side of the lower half of the firmament obliterating the surrounding stars.   Charles' Wain above the cottage is just discernible, but most familiar constellations are absent. " There's husbandry in Heaven ; her candles all are out."

The first disturbance comes from two little owls on a spruce fir behind us.   Their tones suggest that they are young ; so do their manners, for they are quarrelling.   From the depths of the wood a brown owl calls them to be quiet ; they cease their wrangle as though in obedience to the larger bird's note.   The moon gilds the summer-house through the open window and sends little lines of amber through cracks in the wood.

12.15.   A breeze blows chill over the hillside, coats are called for ; the L.A. foresaw the need.   Brown owls still call ; from a far field comes a burst of horrid laughter. Who can be abroad just now ?

12.50.   A rabbit screams ; I recognise the note.   A steel trap has been sprung or a stoat is on its line ; in either case there is no hope of escape.   It is singularly affecting, this cry of despair to the blind, unheeding night ; if I might help this one of hundreds of rabbits that have wasted my fields, I could not hesitate.   But the commonplace tragedy is being con-summated out of reach in some open space beyond my boundaries, among Scotch firs, chestnuts, larches, and brambles.   A prowling cat passes woodwards.   Then I see a ghost ; a shadowy figure appears suddenly in the far meadow.   No, not a ghost, only a white cow that has risen from the grass to stand in the moon's light.

At this moment the fragrance is indescribable.   The breeze has passed over the night-scented stocks and tobacco plants, and when that odour fades one is conscious of the keen, sharp scent of pines.   Shadows on fields are extravagantly long, the definition of tree tops very sharp. I have a feeling that we are intruders upon the peaceful night scene, that Nature does not want onlookers here and now.

1.45. The wraith of Black Brook has attracted another like apparition from above bulrush and iris clumps nearby the spot where the nightingale built her nest when May and April met. A harsh croaking note comes from the wood across the valley; is it a heron calling now? Pheasants are disturbed; several cry out, dogs bark. For a moment night becomes full of anxiety, but the moon insists that all is well and soothes the woods to silence. There is a movement along the wire fence that keeps the garden from invasion. I flash the lamp, there is much scuffling. Rabbits, undeterred by previous failures, are trying to win through.

2.0. Just before us, faintly visible under the shadow of ash and whitethorn is the tiny waterfall, if that be not too big a name for so small a spring. Heat of Summer and frosts of Winter have proved powerless to restrain it. One can only be grateful for a persistence which keeps the great tank responsive to the pump by which the gardener drives water to the hill top to serve his many needs. But over and above the gentle monotone to which a listening ear is so fully attuned, are other sounds, a faint rustling and scraping. I pick up the torch and send a long beam of light along the bank. The hedgehog curls up at once, the brown rat crouches bewildered. I lift the beam for a moment to see beyond, when it is back on the spot, rat has disappeared, hedgehog remains motionless. Something has stirred owls to activity. A ghostlike white one hissed his way along the woodside a moment ago, two brown cousins afar are calling with uncommon energy. I am hoping that the near one will meet the rat as he sails down hill; it is not unlikely; doubtless he knows where creatures of the night come to drink. We owe a lot to owls round here, and only the little owl has paid the heavy penalty demanded of those who help ignorant people.

2.45. Pheasants, suddenly disturbed, are calling anxiously.

3.0. The moon has travelled far across heaven, meadows

are golden, but the mist above the brook takes no colour from them. The fox now crossing from the wood with an easy confident stride is unmistakable. There is just a little touch of haste about his movement; he looks rather like an honest citizen hurrying for a morning train; but in all probability his sole intent is to be away quickly from open spaces. He must have disturbed the roosting pheasants; now, I imagine, he is out after rabbits that will be coming to breakfast in a little while, and may be destined to provide instead of obtaining one. The chill has increased, the L.A., wrapped in her cloak, has dozed off. I think I must have done the same for it is now

5.15. Robin, who keeps me company when I work here by day, has found us both asleep, and from a bramble spray has wakened us with the prettiest matin song in the world. Lady moon is well away on our right, where she will have a magnificent view of the sunrise now nearly two hours away. Wraiths in the valley have joined forces and become one mist.

5.45. Other birds are singing now, wood pigeons plaintively clamorous above their nests, are preparing for an acorn breakfast. A sedge warbler is shrill and brief, a thrush very brief but by no means shrill. Tree-creeper calls as he runs briskly up the nearby elm, some goldfinches on their way to a bunch of upland thistledown are silent; there is nothing to recall the early summer chorus. Cocks are crowing.

6.5. Two sparrow hawks have dashed down upon the flock of finches to make a cruel breakfast. A little later and the transformation scene in the East tells of sunrise. We regain hill top, cottage and kitchen, where the kettle murmurs amiably.

We have left a young sun to disperse mists and warm a very cold countryside for which we have no more immediate use. The moon still clearly visible, " 'gins to pale her in-effectual fires."

8.0. REFLECTION. An uncomfortable night; such past-times as this should cease before middle-age—or be kept for midsummer. We agree that it will be wiser to recom-mend the experience than to repeat it.

93.—Another Kindly Man.

Another kindly man has been to see me since I wrote last.
We have a number of them in these parts. He looked over
the hedge, the sharp-faced, clean-shaven, blue-eyed elderly
philanthropist, and made me a handsome offer.

The K.M. : " You bin busy at yours, Master, ever sin' you
come here, beggin' your pardon."

The Scribe : " There's a lot to do yet, I'm afraid."

The K.M. : " You don't want forever o' vermin about a
place like this. They'll spile it for ye, sure as harvest."

The Scribe : " You're right ; we don't want them."

The K.M. : " Say the word, Master, an' I'll bring me nets
an' ferrets an' clear out all y'r rabbits afore you kin turn
round."

The Scribe : " Thanks, but I couldn't think of troubling
you."

The K.M. (persuasively) : " If there's any owd rats, I'll
ketch 'em too, time I'm seeing arter y'r other things."

The Scribe : ." We haven't many rats, only one now and
again, and the rabbits are wired out of the garden."

The K.M. : " Sarve 'em right ; they ain't no good to
nobody ain't rabbits. They'd eat ye outer house an' home
soon as look at ye. Let me ketch 'em, Master, an' I'll allow
ye a trifle, threepence each, say. I won't leave one on 'em."

The Scribe : " Thanks, but I don't think I want them
caught."

The K.M. (astonished) : " That's a rum un."

The Scribe (apologetically) : " I like to see a few rabbits
about."

The K.M. (baffled) : " Well, if things goo wrong, an' you
git ate up, that on't be my fault, Master. I bin an' warned
ye."

The Scribe : " If I change my mind and want help I'll
remember you, if you'll give me your name and address."

The K.M. : " They don't sinify. Time I'm hereabouts
agen, I'll have a look at ye."   (Exit.)

The Rector told me there used to be a wonderful poacher
in these parts ; he thinks he has gone to another county.
I am wondering if he has returned or has found a successor,

for of the character of my visitor there could be little doubt. I have not lived in the neighbourhood and the occasional company of poachers for more years than the century has known, without recognising them. Perhaps he won't take "no" for an answer. The thought adds spice to the pleasures of country life. How wonderful, how undeserved the kindness of unknown acquaintances, who would not stand by and see you ruined by wild rabbits and will actually pay you (threepence) for each one they can't hide.

When I was younger and more simple I did engage a gentleman to clear some fields near my garden. By dint of stratagem I was able to discover where he cached those he did not speak about, and day by day, when he went home to tea, I retrieved them. He always came back after dark to pick up his profits, and came in vain. In the end when I settled for those he had shown me and told him I did not propose to pay for the others, he told his friends I " hadn't done honest by him, and that I was ' double cunnin'."

CHAPTER XVII

THE YEAR PASSES

94.—November.

November comes too soon; so many of the summer's tasks are incomplete and the lessening of daylight hours is a growing hindrance to work. The townsman doesn't rise early enough to note the change.

At this season we begin to plan for winter. There's a " lawn " to renew, additional garden to prepare, a corner to plant. At first I thought I would be content to wire back all the rabbits, but I found that a couple of acres could well be spared from the grass land and a small warren should prove useful. It was necessary to surround it with strong wire, buried to a depth of eighteen inches and to plant a little gorse and broom for cover, and incidentally for colour. Such a warren will be attractive and should provide a food reserve and a tangible asset, though the country price of rabbits is low.

Apart from garden making, there is considerable transplanting before us. We know by now that some of the soil is too sandy for certain fruit trees and, so soon as the life has died down, we must move a few to ground where there is more loam. On the sandy soil we can plant the things that do not care for water. Heather, broom, *rosa rugosa* and hypericum would be good if the rabbits would suffer them to display their qualities with, perhaps, certain irises.

Now we approach the time when the stock of garden requisites may be replenished cheaply. Wise people who have surplus sell in the Spring when the demand is definite ; wise folk who are short buy in the Autumn if they can wait so long ; the patient follower of sales can gather bargains. Rollers, grass cutters, shears, flower pots, all these find their way to many a saleroom and are sold at prices calculated seriously to annoy the manufacturer. It is only now and again that one attends an overcrowded sale where second-hand material is dearer than new, and then it is safe to say that friends of the seller have attended to push prices. Among my bargains is a motor lawn mower that when overhauled by an expensive but reliable firm of motor engineers cost ten pounds The only drawback to self congratulation is that we haven't enough grass to justify the purchase, indeed grass is no more than a courtesy title for some of the stuff we cut through the early years of our sojourn, even though it is a fair description to-day.

It is perhaps disconcerting to learn that local opinion writes you down an ass, but truth is stubborn and must be faced. I have made a little list and put a mark against the names of six or seven people who have deliberately sought to take advantage of me, not, I think, out of ill-will or ill-feeling, but merely because as one admitted frankly, in the course of a chat that began stormily but ended in friendly fashion, " I don't belong." That a stranger should have any idea of the extent of a fair day's work or its proper value, is regarded as quite unlikely, and if, indeed a fact, a very discreditable one.

" What will you charge me for this job ? " I asked one of those who will not be approached again.

" I'll think it over an' let ye know," he said, adding twenty-four hours later, " that'll be twelve pound."

"I'm sorry," I replied. "I shan't be able to ask you to do it for me."

"Well, there, I haven't been able to measure up," he admitted, "so I may be able to do it for a shade less. I'll go and look." On the following morning the figure had fallen by just half—at which price the work was done by somebody else. There was ample profit in the second sum, even on London rates, which do not obtain in the country, but it seemed good to my neighbour to lose a job by over-pricing it and thereby taking himself out of the range of further tenders. I think it was in "A Pair of Spectacles" that Benjamin Goldfinch, the leading character, says, "if a man cheats me once I cry shame on him, if he cheats me twice, I cry shame on myself."

The placid week-ender whose primary purpose is to fill his lungs with fresh air, originated this kind of trouble. He is simple; there is a race to capture his jobs before he becomes wise; those who are not daring, get left. At the same time, one should not generalise. Within a short distance is a native who has done us a number of good turns, apparently because he expresses a natural kindly disposition in this fashion. A hearty, good-natured man, this, who must work very hard for a living and contrives to bring a smile to each job. One of these will atone for half a dozen unreliables. And there are real country builders who can do anything that requires joiner, carpenter, painter, bricklayer, thatcher, tiler, plasterer or drain layer.

At this season our quiet corner of the world appears to be entirely deserted. When postman, milkman and paper boy have called, we are left alone. I can spend morning and afternoon between summer house, workroom, and garden. Not only there is no news from the outside world, there is no hint that such a world exists, we are as free from association with it as the last insects among ivy blooms and the lark in the sky. Then at six o'clock I go into the study, turn a switch, hear a time signal and learn everything of importance that has happened in the day and is deemed safe for the ordinary citizen to be told.

95.—WRITING WEATHER.

Autumn has changed her mood since last I wrote. She released a south-westerly gale last night, to storm the valley and fling invisible forces at walls and windows as though to test the builder's honesty. Then finding the cottage invulnerable, the gale assailed the garden and wrought its savage will on great dahlias, the gardener's pride, on the last of modest nasturtiums that are mine and the Michaelmas daisies that sounded so gracious a note through October days. Happily the gardener eyes the month with grave suspicion and some of the best of his blooms were securely tied to strong stakes; only a few heavy-headed stems crashed. It was strange to see the struggle of the birds for wing-hold when morning came. "The rooks are blown about the sky," wrote Tennyson, and had he been watching the effects of the gale, he might have added pigeons, starlings and a host of finches. I noticed that jays and magpies never left the wood; there was a welcome absence of gun fire; even partridges had nothing to fear.

In Cornwall and along the Welsh coast a south-west wind brings rain. By the time it has travelled across England it has been compelled to drop all moisture and, feeling dry, is angrier than ever; at least, I think that this would be Mr. Coyle's explanation.

96.—AN OLD FARM.

This afternoon we came upon one of the Elizabethan farm houses of which the countryside is full. The farmer had failed, his "Looker" or bailiff came up while we looked on. Mr. Pink had met losses. "Some big concarn," explained the Looker. "He put the money in it an' that swallowed it, so he got to goo. Bes' master ever a man had, never grumbled at nawthen ne yet nobody. Took the owd farm to the bank time he wanted money, an' now the bank's sold it. A good master, mind ye, I'm clearin' up for him. Tricksy things banks, I don't howd wi' sech meself; ye can't trust 'em rightly. I read a piece in th' paper that ain't so long ago to say we don't want banks. I never had no truck with them meself, but there, there's a many doos seem'ly."

I walked round near fields of the farm; it had been cared for. A steading, thatched and wired on the south face, clean cart bays with well-pointed brick work, a matured garden with espaliers against a south wall and a few young cordons, too young to be in full bearing. Doubtless the owner had hoped to dwell in security, as a dozen generations of farmers have done in the same holding. They had known it in the years when Drake and the Armada met, when Royalist and Parliamentarian fought at Marston Moor or Naseby, when Monmouth's cause was spent in blood on Somerset marshlands or at the Assize of Judge Jeffries, when Napoleon rose and fell and Bismarck established a German Empire.

All those world-shaking events had left the little farm house in the lane completely indifferent, merely because the aeroplane had not reached the plane of manifestation. The dormer windows and twisted chimneys, the buildings through which countless beasts had passed, fertile fields, wherein so many ploughmen had laboured from early manhood till old age, had suffered no change. Now there was just a break in continuity, the farm was untenanted, the garden paths littered with leaves, there were young weeds in flower beds from which they had long been barred.

" It all come very sudden," said the Looker, just as though he had read my thoughts. " Master should ha' told me he reckoned he'd clear hisself, but things went contrairy, an' he never. A good man to work for, mind ye ; nobody heerd him grumble time things went wrong. We'll feel th' miss of him hereabouts."

The farm would welcome a stranger and he, too, must pass in a little while, leaving no trace, perhaps not even gracious memories in the hearts of those who served him.

There had been a brief space of sunshine when we went down the lane, now the gale was bearing masses of cumulus cloud with it and light was dimmed. A flock of plover wheeled in circle round the ploughland, alternatively black and white as they turned, there was something melancholy

PLOVER

in their movement. Dead leaves came whirling by as though to proclaim not only the passing of another year, but the death of a great hope and the failure of an honest endeavour. It would be one of the countless minor tragedies that goes unnoticed, for who save a few tradesmen drove down that quiet lane ? But that we have something of a love for byways and an incurable distaste for main roads, we never had seen the place.

An empty farm house is not so melancholy in the Spring ; there is blossoming time in the most derelict of orchards, wayfaring birds do not pause to ask if the house beyond the garden be tenanted, or empty. But when days are drawing in and wind has taken charge and the plover holds the fields, there comes a sense of depression hard to resist. It needed the sight of the cottage with lights aglow, a cheerful fire and the kettle's lively solo to dispel the gloom. We could not keep inglenook seats in the cottage, they were so draughty, but I have known inglenooks to which nothing but warmth could come, with little hollows to hold a man's mug and glass and pipe, while he sat in comfort and talked to his wife across a welcome blaze.

How simple and pleasant that old life was, outside the homes of the farm labourers, whom the farmers overworked and underpaid; when bread came from bake-oven and beer was brewed in cellar and sides of bacon hung in the chimney and there were pleasant wines made by the housewife from garden fruit or vegetables. Light might have been no more than tallow candles with snuffer or even rushlight, conveniences may have been few and luxuries hard to seek, but there was no standard of comparison that might provoke contrast. If the necessities of life were to be had—food, warmth, shelter—there was ample measure of content. At least, this is what I gathered when I was a lad, talking with very old men and women, small holders who had been born while Napoleon still filled the world with strife and ugly earth-shaking events, and have long passed to their appointed end drawn in double harness by hard work and content.

97.—Preparing for Winter.

I bought a batch of aged hens in Spring for stewing and then moved by compassion for their plight, for they had had very rough handling on their way to and from market, decided to give them an extra summer. They expressed their thanks with a few eggs and then came to table and rewarded me by adding to the sense of self-support, because they went into the pot in company with vegetables they might have seen growing. The store cupboard reveals attractive shelves; tomato sauce and mushroom ketchup are making a first appearance; home-potted meats are in reserve for emergency. I have as we say " spoken for " some country wines. Certain old trees have been cut down to provide material for log fires by which the L.A. and I sit making garden plans for another year; the cottage has been overhauled for winter.

It is a cheerful moment. Autumn pauses, Winter has not shown her cold hand, even though the days shrink they have hours that seem to belong to the sunshine, and birdsong has returned after the late Summer silences.

98.—THE BAT.

" You've not been in the attic," said a friend, the old marshland farmer whose pleasant home was built in years when Philip of Spain was preparing his Armada against these shores. " Go and see how well the beams have stood. You'll be interested."

I went up and saw that the sunrays found a way through the tiles though the rain could never follow it. The oak floor carried signs of hard wear but the roof beams were of the kind that blunts carpenter's nails. The place, I thought, would invite bats to take up their winter quarters. The year was advancing, I had watched pipistrelle's evening flights for days past ; after searching a rather dusty ledge I found one. Sleeping, I thought at first, then lit a match and saw that the little body was shrivelled and as I lifted the light frame gently with one hand to place on the palm of another, it fell to pieces. The bat had gone into winter quarters with as much food as a diminishing store of insect life would yield, it had reduced the life process to a minimum, the gentlest breathing, the smallest waste of tissue ; a race had been run between Time and vitality. Time had conquered and the little ranger of the twilight had passed to the deepest sleep of all, to become a mere shell that would presently crumble into dust. How gently Nature had dealt with its tiny child; why will she not show an equal kindness to her children of a larger growth ?

Squirrels, dormice and other hibernating creatures face like trials, but if squirrels wake in winter they go to a store ; I had seen them moving in the wood in January last and a meal of hazel and Spanish chestnuts would have given immunity for a long time. But should the bat respond to a spell of warm late Autumn sunshine it is in grave danger, for such insect life as persists is dormant. There is no food to be had, while movement and fuller breathing reduce the small store of vitality. Squirrels and birds get the best of our spring, summer and autumn weather, but bats have little more than twilight and darkness. The most they can hope for is sufficient store of insects to take them over to another limited spell of freedom at the price of endless hard work.

99.—NELLY.

THE friendly tradesman said he would be glad to help, so we carried Nelly to his van and made her as comfortable as we could with a bag round her; she always loved to ride in a car; but to-day the interest had gone. It is a six-mile drive to the town where the veterinary surgeon, kindest of men, lives, and in his absence the assistant, who loves dogs, will be on the premises. We may not use our own car to drive her in; this would have been an unauthorised journey.

We have said time and again, when Death has visited the kennels, that we would never keep another dog, and then the utter emptiness of country life without one has turned away the current of what we took for a fixed resolve. Without forgetting friends in our private Pantheon we have sought new ones and have never failed of our reward.

Nelly, the Norfolk Lurcher, came by chance. Driving through the county from which her name derives, I saw a notice, "Dogs For Sale," and called at a tumbledown small-holding where nearly a dozen animals were on offer. Nelly was the only unhappy one among them; so I chose her. "Rabbits!" said her owner. "You only got to show her one, guv'nor, an' she's out arter it an' brought it to ye before you kin turn round. Twenty-five bob, guv'nor, an' dirt cheap. There's many'd ast two pun. You mark me words."

I did mark them, and twenty-four hours later took Nelly to a meadow where, as far as a rapid count could tell, sixty rabbits were in pursuit of health and beauty. I released Nelly and she darted away at a fine pace to the very end of the field. Then she turned round and came back at the same high speed. A few rabbits made haste to get out of her way, but there was no need to do so.

She did not bring me any save baby rabbits, and these she picked up tenderly and brought carefully, sometimes frightened, never hurt. I began to understand why she had not looked happy in the kennels, probably she had been tried and found wanting as a lurcher, or "useful dog," perhaps treated roughly, for she was very nervous until she had been long enough with us to know that her limitations and shortcomings did not count.

Very soon she became the faithful companion, lying patiently at my feet, following closely at my heels, and so full of affection to all the world that she took every man, woman and child for a friend ; never was dog equipped with more placid temperament. When air raids came to the neighbourhood she would be frightened, would seek my room and crouch under my bed, but she never barked or whined. If I went to town for a day or two, she would settle down by my chair so soon as I returned ; this was her nearest approach to being demonstrative.

Nelly soon became part of my life, a part of which I was hardly aware, but so definitely a part that when I attended any local committee meeting, she would follow me to the hall or schoolhouse and keep so quiet that nobody raised any objection.

Through this long, sunny afternoon of mid-winter—something to be grateful for if one knew how—lines by Kipling have been coming back to me :

When the body that lived at your single will

When the whisper of welcome is stilled (how still !)

When the spirit that answered your every mood

Is gone—wherever it goes—for good,

    You will discover how much you care——

These lines, for all their beauty, are a part of the cloud that shuts out the sun.

Occult science declares that there is a constant upward procession of life from mineral to plant, from plant to beast, from beast to human and beyond on a scale of development we are hardly able to comprehend. Students of the occult say that elephant, horse and dog are nearest in evolution to man, and that by the aid of his and their great love given, the gulf may be bridged. This is daring speculation, but who, having loved elephant, horse or dog, will dismiss the belief as unworthy of credence ? " There are more things in heaven and earth, Horatio——"

Our finite mind cannot grasp the Divine Intent but we may be convinced that the love of a man for his dog is something of high significance and is filling a greater purpose than we know, for both Life and Love are in the Divine Gift. On the other hand, the dog's love for his master or mistress, so utterly single-pointed, so utterly indifferent to all worldly standards, is something that cheers, satisfies and enriches.

It is fair to remember that our dogs flatter us. For them we have no faults, we cannot be too poor, too shabby, too disreputable for their affection. They would not leave us for the greatest potentate, the stateliest palace, they are our sworn friends till death do us part. I can't help thinking that Bill Sykes, for all his brutality, must have had a sneaking affection for his dog, even though he sought to destroy it and there can be no doubt about the dog's feelings towards the only human he could look to. Did the dog's affection mean nothing to his master ? I doubt it.

. . . . . .

The vet. has just rung up. Age and dropsy and a weak heart are the troubles, but Nelly is not in pain. If she comes back it will be as an invalid, no more walks up and down the hill on which our home is perched, nothing better than an easing of a road inevitably brief. On the other hand I can ask for swift euthanasia and the end.

" Do everything you can," I told him ; " keep her with you for a few days, and then, if she can be moved, we will fetch her. She has earned the right to die at home." It may be that if he can see her through this trouble she will live long enough to enjoy next summer on the lawn and will sense such friendliness and attention as we should welcome when our turn comes. I hold two firm beliefs, first that all life is one life, differing only in manifestation, and secondly, that we bear a large responsibility to the lives that come under our care. Happily, in this matter, as in all others that really count, the C.O. stands by my side. " Of course, we must have her back," she says.

So we face in our remote corner, and not for the first or even the tenth time in our association now over thirty years old, the sorrow that tears the hearts of all dog lovers and we may ask, with Kipling, why, in a world where there is always trouble for one and all, we should add to it by giving our heart to a dog to tear.

It is a question none can answer, a problem none can solve, and the only difference between Nelly and those that have preceded her lies in a thought that we may no longer replace our pets, since the time is at hand when in the ordinary course of Nature the puppy may well outlive its owner.   Bad as it is for man to lose his dog, something tells him it is worse for the dog to lose his master.   The dog passes, a friend is lost, and other interests help to fill the gap that looks so wide and deep, but if the owner passes, the dog is left alone in the world.

The vet. has just rung up to say that Nelly died in her sleep, just a couple of days after I had called, and she did not recognise me.

I know that the world is full of trouble, but this knowledge does nothing to diminish my sense of loss.

I have turned for consolation in a loneliness that is terribly real to the third chapter of Ecclesiastes : " Who knoweth the spirit of man whether it goeth upward and the spirit of beast whether it goeth downward to the Earth?"

And I remember that when Tobias and the Angel went to Rages of Media, "the young man's dog went with them" and that when they returned "the dog went after them."   Clearly the dog was not deemed unworthy to be in the company of one of the Seven Holy Angels.

A comforting thought, for Tobias could not have had a dog more kind, affectionate and gentle than mine. (Winter 1944-45).

ROBINS FIGHTING

CHAPTER XVIII

SUNDRY TROUBLES

100.—Scandal.

I suppose we grow censorious as we advance in years and though I have no wish to say anything against my neighbours, truth compels me to remark that the first one I met on a recent morning was an overdressed female with a harsh voice who is suspected of being no better than a thief; her character is really very bad. She hurried round the corner so soon as she saw me; they do say about here that she gets up early to steal people's vegetables. Then I met another neighbour who keeps absurd hours; he and his wife quarrel like cat and dog and don't mind who hears them. There's a third on whom I chanced, an impudent fellow who is said to have driven his children away from home last Summer; I have every reason to believe that this is true, and that very few people blame him. They say it was time for the children to fend for themselves.

Mr. Tripp had been complaining of a neighbour, the carpenter, who it appears charged him too much for mending an old chair and said by way of excuse that the wood was rotten. "I towd him that seat served me gran'father an' me father an' me too, so there couldn't be much that's rotten about it," said Mr. Tripp, and went on to tell me of the carpenter's discreditable antecedents and shameless life, how he had tried persistently to help him and was always robbed for his pains, how in future he would not offer him a job, large or small.

Not to be outdone I told Mr. Tripp of my disreputable neighbours and he was at once interested.

"I haven't been up your way these years," he remarked, "but time I goo up next, I'll have a look at 'em. Which are they? I used to know a few folk thereabout."

"I don't think I ought to go so far as to name them," I protested. "I've spoken too freely. It doesn't do to spread scandalous tales."

"You're mostly bound to name 'em," he retorted, "if you bin telling the truth."

Clearly he was interested, he stopped the work he had resumed and leaning on his fork intent upon hearing the names of the offenders, ready if I do him no injustice, to tell me that he had heard of them and could have told me, had I asked, that they were no good.

"Well," I replied, with an appearance of great reluctance, "if you must know, the over-dressed thieving lady is called Mrs. Jay, the couple who start quarrels with daylight are Mr. and Mrs. Sparrow, and the gentleman who drove his young family away is Mr. Robin Redbreast."

There was really no occasion for Mr. Tripp to lose his temper and use what is called "langwidge." Nor was it true to say I had wasted his time. He stopped me to tell of the carpenter's shortcomings.

101.—A SANDY MAN.

"They'll play hemp along o' your grass, Guv'nor," said a voice at my side.

I looked round and saw a little sandy man, who bore some remote resemblance to a ferret. He waved his hand in the direction of the valley meadow where rabbits were eating at my expense.

The Scribe: " It's all right. I've wired against them. Only a few get through."

The Sandy Man: " You don't want no wire, Guv'nor you want a handy man, to set yokes (snares) or lay nets."

The Scribe (evasively): " Some of them come from across the valley."

The Sandy Man (with authority): " Time they're on your land they're yourn, Guv'nor. If anybody sez they ain't, you tell 'em they are. I've took uncommon notice o' rabbits one way or another."

The Scribe: " Yes, I think you take notice of them on my meadows in the early morning, don't you? I generally hear half a dozen reports round about five o'clock in the morning, sometimes a little earlier." This was indeed a shot at venture, but it did not lack effect; my visitor flushed a little and thought for a moment. "Lord love ye, Guv'nor, how you do go on to be sure. That worn't me. That must ha' bin one o' th' men on th' fruit farm. Dedn't oughter be allowed, wakin' honest folk up."

The Scribe: " Were you disturbed? "

The Sandy Man: " I don't b'long round about, Guv'nor. I come from a little way out. But you gimme the word an' I'll clear th' place, so you won't know it. You buy me a gross o' snares an' gimme a quart o' beer a day an' I'll do it f'r ye, an' on'y take th' rabbits. That'll pay me enough to live on; I don't want th' arth, Guv'nor."

The Scribe: " You're the fourth to offer to clear the rabbits. One man offered me threepence a piece, large and small."

The Sandy Man: " He'd never ha' pide it, Guv'nor. He'd ha' let ye down time you ast him f'r your money. There ain't any man can set yokes an' tend 'em to pick up rabbits, an' hire a cart to take 'em to town an' p'y thruppence. I've cleared an uncommon lot o' rabbits in my time: Live and let live, that's my motto, Guv'nor."

The Scribe: " How about the rabbits? "

The Sandy Man: " They don't wanter live. They ain't no better than poachers."

The Scribe : ' I must think it over—your name and address ? "

The Sandy Man : " They don't sinify, Guv'nor. I come round here whiles ; I'll look f'r ye."

The Scribe : " You won't find me about much before seven o'clock. I'm down quite early, but I don't always go out."

The Sandy Man : " I'll bear it in mind, Guv'nor."

He was the second man wearing a coat with game pockets to it who wanted to catch rabbits but did not want to give his name and address.

102.—A TILE OFF.

" His own fault," said Mr. Tripp ; " he ast for it." Some days had passed and he has forgotten that I tried to deceive him.

A mile away and some months earlier, the gale had found its way under the tiles of a very old cottage and had stripped part of the roof. The only available carpenter-handyman had made the best job he could of the necessary repairs, but the tiles did not match, the patch was unsightly, the charm of the little place had gone. We can't afford to lose beauty in the countryside just now, at a time when the speculative jerry builder may choose any attractive site to defile. I said as much to Mr. Tripp and the opening line was his comment.

" He couldn't help himself," I protested, " the winds were terribly severe in the Spring, nothing that wasn't really sound could stand against them."

" I know all about that," replied Mr. Tripp. " If you'd come down here middle of April you could ha' picked up me daffs what the wind had blown the heads off. I wouldn't ha' stopped you ; they weren't worth anything. But old man Taffy deserved all he got."

" Why ? " I asked.

" When he was down here first," Mr. Tripp replied, " he come along here an' saw my houseleek growing on the roof. He ast why I had it. ' If you grow houseleek on your roof th' lightnin' can't strike it, ne yet a thunderbolt,' I told him."

" ' You're superstitious,' he said. ' That's an owd-fashioned notion o' yourn,' he said, just like that. ' That isn't one roof in a million catch the lightnin',' he said."

"What did you tell him?" I asked. I grow houseleek on the cottage roof not because I share the old country belief expressed by Sir Thomas More in the reign of Henry VIII that it is "a sure defensative against thunder," but because it is a pleasantly decorative roof plant, and because in the village I know that the houseleek was grown on cottages that have been destroyed not by lightning or thunderbolts but by the foul copyhold tenure that lived until 1930.

"What did you say," I repeated, for Mr. Tripp had forgotten me in the contemplation of his neighbour's transgressions.

"I said to him," replied the old man, "that he wasn't dead yet, so he got a chance to live long enough to git a bit o' sense in his silly head. 'My roof's all right,' he sez. 'I don't want to take houseleek to it. The roof won't bring the tempest and the houseleek won't keep it away.'"

"And when the baker come along las' March an' told me Taffy's roof been most blown over, I knew that was a judgment on him. If you don't know anything in this world, you don't want to contradict those who do. There's too many folk does that," he said pointedly.

103.—OVERHEARD.

"Huntin' isn't what it was. Too many of these (*i.e.*, condemned) poultry farmers. Nothin' but wire, an' claims. Every old hen a pullet, an' every barn-door fowl a museum piece. Some of them will put a strand of barbed wire across the top of a gate. The big farmers aren't what they were either. They don't hunt nowadays; townsfolk a lot of 'em, spawned by some agricultural college. Some of 'em will tell you they can't afford it; some don't want to see other folk huntin'. Farm hands getting very uppish. They're being spoiled, Wages Boards an' out o' work pay an' half holidays an' all that, eh what?

"I don't know what the County Councils are doin' with their footpath notices over every field that fools think they've a right to walk across. They must keep a lot of lazy beggars wanderin' round looking for trouble. And somebody's got to pay for those boards—they go on the rates for sure. The country isn't what it was when my Uncle had the Hall. He didn't stand any nonsense. If he shut up anythin' it stayed shut, and if a man turned sulky he just threw him out. An' they all respected the old boy. If they behaved themselves he was their friend right enough ; he gave 'em a square deal, but he knew what was good for them better than they did."

" A man's land was his own to do what he thought best with in his day. Men and women who worked on it were his servants, whether they planted the potatoes or peeled 'em in the kitchen, whether they reared the pheasants or waited at table. Uncle wouldn't have had a radical on the place or a non-comformist, and everybody who worked for him had to go to church on Sunday morning. He sat where he could see 'em come in or go out ; you couldn't find his blind eye ; he hadn't one. Went his own way and hadn't any soft soap for anybody. You should have heard him on Death Duties. If he hadn't died before the war, poor old beggar—"

I can't tell you what would have happened, for I wanted to jot down as much as I could of what had gone before and the speaker had moved on out of earshot of the summerhouse in which I sat with a sympathetic friend a little apart from the stress and turmoil of a garden party in a near county. It was good to hear the expression of a viewpoint that is more often held than proclaimed in rural districts where progress is a name and privilege a perquisite.

104.—THE WISDOM OF MR. COYLE.

I remember a far-off occasion when the roof of the workshop leaked; though Mr. Coyle, blacksmith, philosopher and village oracle had been summoned to set the trouble right, his reputation as a handy man being well established. Business must have been slack at the forge for he came along within an hour or two of the summons ; though the sun was shining once more he was not deceived. He looked at the aged building with eyes nothing can escape. " That lets wet," he said almost at once. " That want a special mixture I got by me. Costs a bit extry, mind ye, but time th' roof got my skin on it that'll be right as rine." On the following morning the expert was on the job and in a fortunate hour, for his labours were followed by three weeks of dry weather. " That's a bit expensive," Mr. Coyle admitted, when he presented the bill, " but me skin's on that roof and time Josh Coyle done a job that's done and I don't mind who hears me say it." It is perhaps unfortunate that the Clerk of the weather must have been listening in. During the following night the drought broke and so did Mr. Coyle's " skin," the patent rainproof article that costs big money. Its fallability stood revealed beyond doubt.

I am glad to be able to record that Mr. Coyle received the bad tidings with equanimity. " That was the drought got through it," he explained cryptically, " rain couldn't ha' done it."

" Well, anyway, I'd like it set right at once," I told him, but the wise man held up a warning hand. " I dussn't put it on wet," he explained. " We shall have to wait for fine weather. If I was to put me skin on that, time it's so much as damp, that wouldn't keep the wet out. Josh Coyle don't do jobs like that. You got to wait for a week's fine weather and I'll come an' set it to rights for you, so that'll be sound as if it was thatch."

I found it necessary to put the tools in the shed under a tarpaulin as the roof had continued to " let wet," a little uncertain of Mr. Coyle's ability to intervene very presently and put a term to such behaviour. It seemed hard in these circumstances to justify the impatience of a friend who knew of the episode, or the coarse terms he used in speaking of the handyman philosopher. I reminded him that he who calls his neighbour a fool is in danger of hell fire, but he did not withdraw the dangerous criticism.

OUTBUILDINGS OF A MARSHLAND COTTAGE

CHAPTER XIX

RETROSPECT

105.—CHANGE.

WHEN I spent my first winter in the country, an emancipated law student with a passion for sport, the winter dullness was of a kind that would be regarded as incredible to-day. For wealthy folk who could shoot, hunt and entertain there was no enemy save bad weather, but for the rank and file, the aspect of winter was altogether different. Transport was by dogcart, bicycle or horseback, telephones were not found in rural areas—where I lived second post letters and the daily paper were left at the inn, rather more than a mile away shortly after 2 p.m. There were no lights by the roadside though there were ruts that might splash you from head to heel; oil fed the lamps, grocer called once a week, baker three times. Coal was delivered by the hundred-weight at high prices, persuasion was needed to secure so much as a quarter of a ton at once unless you could hire a farm wagon and have a truck of coal sent to the station six miles away, a big financial operation and impossible in any event for those who had no more than a small coal shed.

There was no place of assembly—Village Hall and Women's Institute were unborn, men had the alehouse tap-room with sanded floor and wooden benches, their wives had nothing but hard work seven days a week for their portion. There was no statutory wage for farm hands, merely a customary one and when very bad weather came along, they lost time. It was no uncommon experience for a farm worker with wife and family to have no more than five shillings to take when Friday night came round. Then the father and mother had to " make do." " I've known father go to work without breakfast many's the day," my old gardener told me, " so that his slice of bread could be cut up for us."

Nowadays you find wireless or gramophone in the smallest cottage, and the man in a job takes home a goodly sum at the end of the week, wet or fine, and there is some meeting-place outside the ale house. " Life is more joyful, Comrades."

" Cunnin' mucks th' Govinment," said my aged gossip

and neighbour across the river when Old Age Pensions came
in.   "Here am I in me seventy-six and you got to have it time
you're seventy.   Do you go up to the Postmaster an' ast
him to gimme what they owe me."

Later he appealed in person to that official and ended up
by saying " I doubt you bin an' kep' it in y'r own pocket.
Don't tell me.   If I was young enough I'd larn ye, but there,
me fistses are shrunk cruel."

106.—COOKS.

Where are the cooks of yester year ?   Last week I visited
an old friend who has modernised his house, he is what is
called a yeoman farmer, keen on sport, and a good judge of
stock.   He took me through the kitchen and showed me the
larder.   There must have been scores of packets, soup, meat,
poultry, vegetables, all in tins.

" What would your Mother have said to this collection ? "
I asked.

" Doesn't do to think," he replied.   " She kept the old
store room filled and everything there was her making or she'd
seen it made under her eye."

" It was all labour of love," he went on, " wines, cordials,
ointments, as well as potted things.   The hams came to
table from the chimney and she never minded how many folk
dad brought in to dinner or supper.   I've heard him admit
that he never could take her by surprise.   Her mother, my
grandmother, ran a still-room.   Mother couldn't go quite
as far because she hadn't the time, there were half a dozen
of us to bring up."

Late that evening as we sat over the fire he took up the
thread of the morning's discourse.

" We've changed everything," his sister said ;   she keeps
house for him.   " As things are we've no provision for large
scale bread making and bacon curing and the rest of it.   But
against that," she went on, " the old kitchen slavery has
gone.   It takes half the time to cook dinner to-day and with
electric stoves and modern washing gadgets, Mary says things
run like clockwork.   If only we were nearer a cinema we could
keep all the maids we want.   As it is we just manage to carry
on by aid of the wireless."

Only those who can remember the old conditions of hard labour in the country house can realise the extent of the change. It has been so great that while to-day a maid is as precious as a pearl of great price, the other generation of housewives could pick and choose from the girls brought by mothers anxious to find them a place where they would get fair treatment, enough to eat and a small wage.

107.—Good Old Times.

" When I was a little old boy," said Mr. Tripp, " folk worked. They worn't afraid of a job."

" Most of them work to-day if they get half a chance," I replied. " Thousands spend the day looking for one." (This was said some years before the war).

" Don't you believe it," cried Mr. Tripp. " My father told me that time he was young, his master'd blow the harvest horn at half pas' fower an' men'd be in the barn ready to start by five. Then they'd keep it up till eight at night. He got a harvest horn an' left it to me brother, so you'll know I'm telling the truth.

" An' I got a brother who was a gamekeeper," continued Mr. Tripp. " Time he brought the young pheasants away from the hens an' put 'em in the woods afore they could perch, he'd go through the woods night arter night blowin' that owd horn to skeer the foxes. He didn't hardly get no sleep an' his money was only fifteen then. If you was to ask folk to do sech things now, they'd talk about a eight hour day."

" But father used to say they were good times," he went on after a pause for breath. " Fat pork fourpence a poun', half a pint o' beer f'r a penny an' th' quart'n loaf fippence. Now you got to pay fippence a pint f'r beer an' your pork will cost a shilling or more, an' loaf as much agen as it did."

" What did your father earn ? " I asked him.

" Twelve," said Mr. Tripp.

" Did you always get enough to eat ? " I enquired.

" Most days," he replied, a little hesitantly perhaps.

" There were times we dedn't. But this house belonged to us and we grew a lot o' stuff."

" Did your father get an Old Age Pension ? "

" He went off dead afore he was old enough," said Mr. Tripp. " He'd ha' took it right enough if so be he could ha' done."

" Nowadays he'd take a far better wage, wet or fine, and some harvest money and get his pension when he couldn't work any more. Don't you think he'd have been better off ? "

" That don't sinify what I think," Mr. Tripp replied. " I dedn't live then, no more dedn't you. But Father did, an' he allus said they wore good old times."

" If you were working on the land would you change them for now ? " I asked him.

" I'd try 'em first an' then I'd tell ye," said Mr. Tripp cautiously. " You can't catch me ; you ain't clever enough."

I wonder if I had set him thinking about the hard facts of those " good old times." Save for a few brave souls whose pluck no adversity could touch, they were times of which all who were responsible, directly or indirectly, have every reason to be ashamed.

108.—In Times Past.

It is easy to cast one's mind back a century or so to picture the gamekeeper at home in our cottage. His " larder " or " gibbet " often a testimony to the ignorance and prejudice of the time, would be nearby. He would work for the Squire (there is no trace of one here ; with few exceptions my neighbours are people of yesterday or the day before), and this work would be long in summer when he had to preserve young and helpless pheasants while refraining from reprisals against foxes. How often would he go through woods by night when the birds were not yet fit to fly, armed with a horn and accompanied by at least another horn blower, their small-hour duty to frighten vermin away ? It is not difficult to see, though it be but as in a glass darkly, lives that came and went in the lone cottage by the wood, and for some reason I would be puzzled to justify, I think that, on the whole, they were happy, that no great upheavals disfigured them.

The tiny place has its own atmosphere, a pleasant one and friendly; if you are sensitive to atmosphere you will feel this at once. It looks out across a lively brook fringed with stately alders to the wood in which a few great oaks were left when war called for the violation of so many sanctuaries; the wood itself still welcomes visitors who do not find happiness in killing bird or beast. It is very nearly a sanctuary to-day; if I could have my way no gun would be heard. But a respected neighbour and friend says, "everybody round here is making up parties to shoot the woodpigeons, they are doing dreadful damage. If your wood is not covered they'll all fly in there and raid the country as soon as the guns are quiet. The Ministry of Agriculture urges us to hold these drives," he goes on, and I feel that I have a public duty that runs counter to my own desires. I won't shoot again, but I agree to allow a couple of guns to help the drive.

109.—FAR FROM THE MADDING CROWD.

There has, I think, been little bird-nesting or trapping here, for wild life of tree and hedgerow dwells unsuspicious and content. A stream trickles down to the woodside to join the brook by way of a shallow pool. Here all manner of rare birds come; some stay to build in the bulrushes, flags and nettles. It would seem as though the place had enjoyed a long spell of peace; perhaps when the keeper's gun woke echoes to deal death to hawk or jay, stoat or weasel, the momentary disturbance seemed but a small price to pay for the destruction of some implacable foe. Of course, there would have been the usual slaughter of pheasants from early November to late January; I only put a period to that a few years ago.

What I would like to understand is whether familiarity bred indifference. For those of us to whom great cities have been a temporary necessity and the country a luxury, there is enduring joy in sylvan surroundings. When I see sedgewarbler, nuthatch, marsh tit, gold crest, hawfinch to-day they bring a thrill; I still watch the tree creeper or listen to the woodpecker hammering and shouting in the wood or follow the longtailed tits at their play, but my struggle for the complete liberty of the country lasted more than twenty-five years. Much self-denial was involved through the season when it was hard to scorn delights for I had a country cottage when just out of my teens, and the joy of leaving London for the week-end was perhaps the keenest in my life.

"You don't wanter come traipsin' up an' down," said my old neighbour and critic of those days. "If Lunnon's all right, stay there. An' if it ain't all right, stay here. You don't belong nowheres by the good rights."

There is no tradition here. We are not living in a country of great estates that have been handed down from Tudor or Stuart times; records are to seek. On the other hand in the absence of well established facts, surmise may be reasonable. I fill my mental gallery of gamekeeping men and their families with portraits of well-spoken, knowledgeable woodlanders, their wives patient and thrifty, their boys and girls honest and courteous, all conscious that their lives are cast in pleasant places and that they share many of the landlord's privileges with few responsibilities. For if we think of it, the gamekeeper whose position is safe, is in a sense a more real owner of woodlands than the man who employs him. He has no other duty than to put a good head of game over or in front of the guns; the largest of life's problems can hardly follow him to the woods; he can enjoy much that his master may find no time to see.

Across the valley my neighbour had an elderly keeper, my tenant now, skilled in all his work, a widower to whom trouble has come bearing many ill gifts. He is quietly content, full of the lore of the woods, patient and resigned; he and I pause to gossip. How much of his content is due to his surroundings, I wonder? Had he been a townsman he could hardly have mingled so much resignation and contentment with his pain; he could not have chosen just the hours when he was feeling at his best to make a garden grow, for in all probability there would have been no garden to hand.

110.—A Link With the Past.

Down to 1933 this cottage had dwelt on no terms with modernity. Its kitchen, living room, two bedrooms and two attics proclaimed much modesty of original purpose. When gamekeepers lived here first, man-traps and spring guns were probably in common use, penal servitude with transportation was the penalty for night poaching. The forgotten keepers may well have been better off than most, for in a dry land and thirsty there are springs that seem unfailing, the air is of the best, walls are thick enough to keep storms out and warmth in. In Summer, rabbits might have been a sore trial to the vegetable garden, deeply buried wire is required to keep them out to-day, but there would have been no lack of meat for the pot. Pigeons must have loved the fir trees then as they do now, there would have been a few fish in the brook and a considerable number of eels.

And all round the woods there would have been cultivated fields with farm houses at long intervals, the carrier's cart the one public medium of communication between distant town and far-flung village.

The cause of the scattered state goes back to the year of the Great Plague of London. It spread to the village and the people scattered. To-day there is only one house near the church and by the road the rectory must be more than half a mile away.

It is possible to take a four-mile walk without leaving the village but the total population is well under a thousand.

The effect of the Black Death and the Plague of 1665 on village life is not fully known ; there is still room for a painstaking investigator. The small forlorn churches of East Anglia can speak selectly but eloquently of the passing of population.

111.—A Contrast.

On this cold and dreary night when winter sat enthroned over a world filled with darkness, frost and fog, I turned over some of the diaries I have kept since I was in my teens. One of these recalls February days spent in the first cottage I

AN ELIZABETHAN COTTAGE

ever rented, a tiny affair of weather boarding, tiles, oak beams
and oak floors, set in a field at the far end of what is called a
green lane, down which at that time of year you walked in
strong heavy boots that had been dressed with mutton fat.
The sodden clay gripped, it was a nasty half mile from the
point where the carrier set you down, unless he had time to
come to the cottage by an upper road two miles out of his way.
The cottage was dependent on oil lamps, one stored oil and
coal before the roads made going too heavy for a single horse
cart. Tradesmen did not call, the place was remote from
the main track, you fetched milk in a jug and water in a
40-gallon tank on wheels from the nearest farm three fields
away. It was necessary to hire the carrier for the journey when
coming from London, because you brought all essential stores
then and kept them in two tin trunks out of the way of mice.
Yet my diary records a happy week snatched from London
in the first days of the snowdrops.

To-night as I write in a cottage equally remote from towns, electric light defies darkness, hot water pipes help log fires to keep rooms warm, the supply of hot water will meet all demands of the bathroom, tradesmen arrive in motor vans, telephone stands on desk. I have not been alone. Orchestras from concert halls and singers from an opera house have kept me company, a well informed gentleman has told me the most important happenings of the day ; from his office in London, an editor has talked for a few moments, from a northern county an old friend. What wonder if the faded diary appears to come out of another world as well as another century ?

The only comparison that favours the Victorian days is concerned with the countryside itself. There is no comparison between the peace, tranquillity, and remoteness of the marshland village that was my home and the place that bears the same name to-day and has nothing else in common with it save the splendid air which does not differentiate between the present hybrids and earlier native population. With the old fondness it cools them in the summer and with like harshness will blow them off the road in the worst of the winter months.

" Give over, darn ye ! " How often have I heard a farm labourer address the east wind in these harsh terms, as I walked a little way with him along the home road.

112.—REFLECTION.

When I read books about country life and gardening I am struck by the fact that I possess a quality—or is it a defect ? —that no other writers share. They cut lawns, they prune trees, they hoe beds, they plant all desirable things in due season, but they never tire. They do not seek garden seat, bench or summer house to reflect with what resignation they may that their long day draws to a late afternoon. I do, and I can assure you that the thought is not altogether an unhappy one. Garden and orchard may be calling on all sides, willing hands may be labouring to gather this or prepare for next year's harvest   flowers, shrubs, vegetables, glass houses may be crying for water just at the moment when you realise that your energy is spent. If you ask yourself why, the answer is merely one of dates.

I paused the other afternoon to reflect upon days when I went to fields of the farmer whose shooting I rented, just to work with the hoe, for very joy of hard labour. I would toil all day long in the hay field, making and shaking out grass, building cocks, loading wains, driving the horse rake. And so far as mere grass cutting is concerned the L.A. and I kept our mile of grass paths in good order, working between breakfast and lunch and from lunch to tea time two days a week. Now, a couple of hours given to fairly strenuous labour compel a rest.

This never happens to the writers of country books. They are robust, vigorous and virile from dawn to dark yet I think the time will come when they will enjoy (?) this crowning experience, when the spirit will be as willing as heretofore, and the body will proclaim its limitations. Then if they be well advised, they will do as I do and reflect gratefully upon the years when perhaps a farmer said to them as one said to me, " You've no call to be ashamed o' y'r day's work."

I had been hoeing turnips for him because he was short-handed, and in common honesty I should add that I charged him nothing for my labours, having a proper sense of their market value.

As a sound farmer he knew that at least as well as I did, and he paid with a word of appreciation that may well have been genuine, for something is better than nothing, and he could spare nobody to help what he called " they turnups."

Like the rest of the world I have received testimonials, doubtless many of them were undeserved and are properly forgotten or set aside, but this one lingers long after " Master Jacob," as the farmer who presented it was called, has gone to his well-earned rest.

113.—Mr. Tripp's Views.

If you go into Suffolk byways where Mr. Tripp dwells, vigilant and well content, it is not hard to realise what life was like in rural England, for Suffolk has no outstanding industries. She is agricultural from end to end. Time was when England outside the immediate area of the towns was in like state, self supplying and satisfied. Then, so far as one can tell, there were few crises. Suffolk in the east, Dorset in the west and Westmorland in the north are, I think, the three counties left to us in which the writ of Nature still runs. In these uneventful areas son has succeeded father. Generation after generation has dwelt in the same farm house, accepting the limited horizons and happy in the limitation.

Mr. Tripp has a stock of traditions, incidentally I might remark that he has draught-proof inglenooks ; I asked him whether he thought that the old folk were happier than their grandsons.

" In course they were," he replied. " They had all they wanted, an' they never heard of anything else. They didn't have newspapers, ne yet books. They taught themselves gardening an' carpenting an' all manner o' things. My father could graft an' bud an' he built his own greenhousen. He dug his own well and bricked it. My mother made all our medicine for coughs and colds and sech. They never saw a train ne yet a sharrybang. They stayed where the good Lord put 'em an' learned to fend for themselves.

CHAPTER XX

THE CHANGING YEARS

114.—Mr. Coyle's Way.

Some years must have passed since I found Mr. Coyle in receipt of custom when I stopped at his forge, but that custom, for the time being at least, was slack and his mature intelligence was free to turn from the making and fitting of horse shoes and the patching of over-worked machinery.

" Time I see ye come up street," said the Master, " I sez ' he'll look in and see me, that's likely.' But you never. Most folk what goo up there (he indicated reproachfully to the direction of my friend's house) come an' chat along o' Josh Coyle if that's on'y for a few minutes."

The Scribe : " I suppose you've always something to tell them ? "

Mr. Coyle (with modest conviction) : " I doubt they wouldn't come if I hand't got anythin' to say. Time you bin an' lived here man an' boy as long as I have, you onderstand men an' women as well as if they bin horses."

The Scribe (to give the necessary lead) : " We do need to understand folk nowadays ; the world's full of trouble."

Mr. Coyle (well started) : " That's a true word. Most everybody got a peck o' trouble to carry about. Serve 'em right mos' times. They shouldn't go on as they do. Then things'd be shipshape. There's a man bin an' come up here that ain't a week ago. ' Come an' have a look at me old thrarshin' machine, afore I want her, Master Coyle,' he sez ; ' she went contrairy last harvest.' So I up an' went down to his, and looked the owd machine straight in th' face. Time I'd seen to a rod an' fixed a nut or two an' put in a couple o' bolts she went as sweet as syrup. That's what you got to do along of anything what bin an' gone wrong. Take it to pieces and fix it up proper. There's on'y one way o' treatin' things, an' that's my way."

The Scribe : " And what is your way ? "

Mr. Coyle : " The right way. There can't be no other nowhere, nohow."

The Scribe : " How would you deal with unemployment for example, Master Coyle ? "

Mr. Coyle (confidently) : " I'd set folk to work."

The Scribe : " What work ? "

Mr. Coyle : " Food growin' to be sure. Parson sez there's bin 300 acres in th' parish gone down to grass in the last ten years. Break it up, sow corn and pertaters. I should ha' read a piece in th' paper what said folk ain't gettin' enough to eat. Why, anybody could come down here an' grow a thousand quarters o' wheat an' five hund'ed ton o' pertaters. When you got all that food in y'r stummick," concluded Mr. Coyle, " you dussn't goo about an' say you ain't had enough to eat."

The Scribe : " I agree. I'll go further ; I believe the time will come when people will do what you suggest. What else would you do to help ? "

Mr. Coyle (firmly) : " I'd stop moty cars and moty bikes an' tractors and sech. Everybody's in too much of a hurry nowadays. Time th' gentry an' th' farmers kep' horses, we dedn't kill folk every time they went out, an' we dedn't have no unemployed. A man don't wanter git killed in th' roadway, time he's lookin' f'r a job. I sez to me friends in th' Dog that ain't a week till Saturday—' Gimme three months' I sez, ' and let Josh Coyle have his own way along o' things, an' if he ain't put 'em to right be then, don't you never b'lieve in him no more.' "

To the best of my belief the offer is still open.

115.—BARNSTORMERS.

Not so many years ago barnstormers came to remote villages, stayed for three nights or six, lived with some modest approach to comfort, and won a frugal living. No cinema existed to compete with them ; they presented virtue triumphant and vice rebuked ; they presented farces that were said to scream. Nowadays they may hope to find at their disposal a village hall complete with stage ; farm workers are better off than they have ever been, there is a demand for amusement. So when I read notices in the village shortly after we came here that the East Anglian Thespians were about to give a week of drama to include *Mona*, " a Manx play," *Jerry the Tramp*, " a moving drama," *Dawn*, " the story of Nurse Cavell," *Other Men's Wives*, " a play for adults only," and finally, *Maria Martin or the Murder in the Red Barn*, I was properly thrilled. There was the further lure of screaming farce and popular prices, one shilling the best, sevenpence the others, tax included. Drama was within my reach. I could go all through the week without threat to the Sunday joint.

There came a sudden summons to town, cutting out the first three performances, but on my return I drove at once to the village hall to find out the hour of the evening show. The place was deserted. " I see them gooin' off in their van this mornin'," said the old countryman who was smoking in his garden nearby. " They ain't had no luck, seen'ly. Folk don't care much about the theayter hereabouts. I never bin to sech a thing all me born days and I ouldn't like I should. T'aint seem'ly."

I made enquiry; clearly my neighbour's conjecture was right. The first house had been poor, the second worse, so bad that money was returned and the players did not proceed to performance. Yet had they stayed there would have been a pleasant change. I met several people who were going to the performance " for adults only," and one or two week-end parties had been planned for Maria Martin, perhaps because the famous Red Barn where the crime was committed is said to be at Polstead over the Suffolk border only a few miles away. It is not, but this is a small matter; it stood there down to a few years ago.

How depressing to think of half a dozen men and women, practised entertainers, driving from the scene of a failure that reflected no discredit upon them. The " beggarly array of empty benches " merely testified to the strength of rival attractions, the garden, the allotment, the wireless set. I think the Thespians should have canvassed the village first after the manner practised by Mr. Vincent Crummles, who knew his business.

Barnstormers are passing from our midst; we ought to do something to maintain their few surviving companies. All of us who are middle-aged or elderly and have lived in the heart of the country owe them something for entertainment in years when they helped village fairs to provide a break in the normal monotony.

116.—HOSPITAL.

The morning called me far afield to find Gammar Ash, who is one of my gossips, walking slowly along her garden path with the aid of two sticks.

" I happened of an illness nigh a couple o' months ago," she explained, " an' they took me to hospital. I on'y been back a fortnight. That's a rum un," continued Gammer Ash, " that on'y take a few minutes to cut ye about, an' ever so long to put ye together agen. I lay on me bed of sickness a month if that wasn't five week."

She had reached the garden seat by now and sat down gladly, very content to bask in the sunshine.

" What do you think of hospital ? " I asked her, knowing the fear and horror that inspire so many simple country folk to whom such a place is no more than a name. How the Wise Men and Wise Women of a past generation used to prey upon the fear of operations and kill sufferers with herbs of healing. Yes, that is not too much to say, for they would continue treatment until the doctor's task was hopeless.

The old lady's wrinkled face lit up with smiles.

" Best place I ever was in all me life," she assured me. " A nice comf'able bed, reg'lar wittles cooked for ye, nothin' to do 'cept to lay still an' listen. They put things over y'r head," she explained, " an' you kin hear a band of music or a prayer meetin' or somebody chatterin' about somethin'. Then folk come in an' talk to ye whiles, just as if you acquainted with 'em. They don't ask you who you may be or where you come from, they jest ask if you're comfortable. Wunnerful frien'ly to my thinkin'."

" Did you suffer much ? " I enquired.

" Not all that much," replied Gammer Ash. " That hurt me where they cut me, an' th' nurses should say they got to keep on interferin' with it ; they never give it no peace. But there, they only puggled it about twice a day an' they done it careful as they could; I ain't got a word agen 'em. I'm sure they done their best an' they never charged me nawthen, but I hadn't anything to pay 'em with, mind ye."

" It's a nice place to be in is a hospital," she continued. " I'd go back agen to-morrow ; folk never done so much for me in all me born days. I never bin waited on before, I've allus had the washin' an' the cookin' and the cleanin' to do."

" That's a change," added Gammer Ash, " and a woman wants a change now and agen. I've known a lot o' folk in me life who'd have bin the better for a month in hospital."

" Operation and all ? " I enquired.

" You can't get in there unless you ail something," explained Gammer Ash, " but I reckon it's worth it. An' you don't know how much you like y'r own home till you bin away from it."

117.—THE WIRELESS.

In populous centres, where you have great choice of distraction, the wireless may mean little to you ; here between the woods it assumes not only importance but all the quality of a mystery. Nearly three hundred years must have passed since somebody built this cottage, perhaps to become its first tenant, and in all probability the wireless was never installed until the summer of 1933 came to the land. Certainly the telephone had not been here before, nor electricity to light lamps, pump water and heat the stove without any call to the hard labour that past generations had to suffer. Commonplaces nowadays, I admit a little later, when I turn another handle and hear the Symphony concert-goers applauding the conductor as he moves to his desk, but yet how wonderful. When we lose our sense of wonder half our pleasure of life must go with it.

There is room for diverse opinions, even here. I went to see an old countryman who has inherited a welcome sum of money by a relative's death. He asked me to come into his ample garden and see what he proposed to do. He intends to have a pig sty, some lights, two fowl houses.

"They will keep me busy between 'em most all the day, he said, "it's only in winter the nights are a bit lonesome." He is a widower.

"Why don't you have a wireless," I suggested, and he shook his head vigorously.

"I don't howd with 'em," he said, and refused to consider the matter. "If my pore owd father bin alive," he concluded after long argument, "he'd have said he didn't howd with sech things, an' if me mother bin alive, she'd have been proper frightened. You never kin tell what one o' them things will say next. I reckon it's safer to be without one. Tell ye the real truth I don't know how it's all done."

118.—COUNCIL HOUSES.

Mrs. Gaymer lives in a thatched Tudor cottage complete with porch and ingle-nook fireplaces of which one has been built in to take a modern kitchener; she can boast dormer windows, and plenty of old oak, some of it in excellent order. Mrs. Gaymer keeps her bees in old-fashioned skeps with shallow frames on top; she sold us honey. In an evil hour I remarked upon the beauty of her home, the seclusion and restfulness of the place; I stood rebuked.

"There's a many sez much th' same thing," replied Mrs. Gaymer scornfully, "but gimme one o' them Council Housen every time. I like a place where ye kin turn round "—the last two words were spoken with capital letters. "I like a place what let th' sun in an' got good-sized winders. I don't like these owd-fashioned places. Why, th' landlord on't let us cut th' ivory." (I discovered on investigation that Mrs. Gaymer meant ivy.) Feeling that sympathy was expected I expressed a proper horror, even while not really sympathising with the lady; small-talk tends to make hypocrites of us all.

"The sparrers keep on buildin' in it an' there's whiles a rat climb up it," she continued, "an' th' tradesmen grumble 'cause they got to walk all along th' garden that time it's wet, an' th' rooms is that low that our boy what's at sea crack his head agin 'em reg'lar. His langwidge! I dunno where he git it from. We never taught him; they must ha' larnt him aboard ship. But there, I like room to swing a cat."

" I'm sure no cat would like it," I urged.

" That's on'y same as a manner o' speakin'," explained Mrs. Gaymer. " I ouldn't swing Rachel," she added, pointing to the tabby cat that sunned herself in the porch, " not if you gimme a pocketful o' suverins. But, mind you, if ever you want to get a cottage, goo to th' Council."

Down on the marshes a few weeks ago I called on a good woman who looked after my cottage long years ago.   She is a grandmother today, and the proud tenant of a Council house. The attractive thatched and beamed cottage in which she lived with her husband when I knew them first has been condemned and pulled down.

" I like meself here," she told me, " but Bill still dolours about the old place.   He should say he'd like to have it back agen an' take th' owd cowl to th' bottom o' th' lane to fetch th' water an' have his garden an' his pigsty in it.   They don't let you keep a pig in the garden nowadays ; that's a dirty bit o' 'em.   If Bill got a pig, he ouldn't mind so much, a pig an' a bit o' extry garden.   He should say all this here's too fashionable f'r th' likes o' him."

" You like it better ? " I queried.

" Ever so much," she replied, " a place may be ever so ill-convenient an' a man on't hardly notice it.   You see he on'y comes in to have his tea an' goo to bed.   An' a woman likes a nex' door neighbour or two," she went on.   " She's at home all day unless she got to goo up street, but a man got his mates to talk to."

It was at least possible to glimpse the two view points. But why, if people are so fond of company do they disfigure companionship with petty quarrels ? Judging by the disputes that come to petty sessional courts from ladies in Council houses, it is possible to have neighbours without adding to the harmony of life.

119.—THE LURE OF THE TOWN.

I was going to London by road when in Stratford I met a big simple son of the marshes whom I had known when I lived there.   Recognition was mutual, we stayed to chat.   He told me he was employed in Spitafields market and earning better money than the land could have brought him.

" Are you satisfied to have left Meadowbank behind ? " I asked him, and was surprised to see how his face flushed at the sound of the familiar name.

" No," he whispered, " I ain't, an' that's th' truth.   I'd liefer be back there agen.   I got me house an' me fowerty rod o' garden an' I liked meself.   Here we've two rooms an' they cost ye forever o' money an' not a mite o' garden. I ain't ate a weg'able sin' I come to Lunnon, leastaways not one that tasted right."

" Why don't you go back," I asked him.   " Farmers are crying out that they can't get enough men ; the land's starved of labour and you look as strong as ever."

" Emmie ouldn't hear on't," he said, his voice still carefully controlled.   " She likes the shops an' th' pichers, an' th' market.   I ast her if she'd come back many's th' time, but she sez she on't be buried alive agin if she knows it.   A man can't fend f'r hisself without his wife," he added by way of explanation, " but if she'd come, I'd giv' master me week right away an' drop th' extr' money.   There's others like me, hereabouts.   They'd goo back if so be they could, but their wimmenkind on't let 'em, seemly.   Wimmen," he added sorrowfully, " are rum 'uns."

120.—Mr. Tripp, Junior.

Mr. Tripp is busy, " all over behind along of me work," he told me when I paused by his gate.   He was double-digging for his vegetables.

" You've a nice show of flowers," I said.

" I don't think nothin' to flowers," he replied.   " Grow theirselves, they do.   But vegetables want thinking about."

" What are folk doin' up in Lunnon ? " he enquired suddenly, as he shook the earth off a big dock root and threw it on a pile that will doubtless provide a bonfire.

" I haven't an idea," I replied.

" I don't suppose they're up to any good," he remarked a little harshly.   " I ouldn't trust any what lives there."

" Ever been to London ? " I asked him.

" T'ain't likely," he replied sharply.   " But I got me boy up there.   I dessay you'll ha' met him.   Islington's the name o' th' part.   He's middlin' short an' his hair's brown, an' he's in the milk business ; goes round with bottles most every day of his life."

When I expressed a fear that I had missed what would undoubtedly have been a pleasure, his father turned on his heel with a gesture that might have been impatience or disgust. Have you shared my experience that every real countryman, who does not know London but has a relative there, is surprised to hear you say you have not met him?

121.—GOING, GOING . . .

The effect of change upon the countryside I know best has been profound.   Men and women do not wish to see their boys and girls on the land, or in local domestic service, and the children are equally unwilling to stay.   Only the old people, bewildered by the incursion of bungalows, Council houses, strangers, electric light, stand pipes, local regulations, and the rest of the upheaval of the later years, are a little frightened or indignant, and more retiring than ever.   To them it appears an intolerable abuse of power by the county or rural district surveyor to condemn the thatched cottage that sheltered past generations before the first surveyor was born.   Then again, the community spirit has been forced upon many who did not desire to hold any intercourse with it.

" You don't belong to yourself no more," complained an old countrywoman to the writer, " along these here clubs. Everybody kin go to the one up street.   Time I went there I found ——— and ———, dollops each o' th' both of 'em. I never did acquaint along of 'em all me born days.   An' them wireless folks comin' inter y'r room and talkin' to ye, just as if they belonged.   That can't be right.   An' moty cars comin' along all time o' th' day an' night ; it ain't safe to cross the road without you wanter be knocked down."

I sought for other expressions of this attitude, doomed to disappear with the countryside of which it was a part and when found, either on the Essex Marshes, or in Suffolk villages, seldom in my colourless immediate neighbourhood, I have jotted them down, recognising that we cannot retrace life's milestones, and what is once lost is lost for ever. It has been my fortune to witness the passing of the countryman of Essex and East Anglia, the pace of the builder's progress, the passing of individuals beneath the steam-roller of drab uniformity, driven by men whose virtues are unstained by imagination.

Perhaps the most serious loss has been the passing of the village craftsmen. The modern farm worker cannot dig a drain or layer a hedge, or thatch a stack with the old-time ease and certainty, the mechanisation of the farm with its tractors, harvester combines, driers, and the rest, has made this individual effort unnecessary or superfluous. The village bootmaker has gone and the " bake oven " fed with faggots has lain cold for years, the village craftsman has been driven out by the machine, and the life of the village is regulated by the big urban store. Wheelwright and blacksmith are passing, or have passed, the bee-master is hard to find. Even the village carpenter may find his occupation gone and you may look near and far and vainly for the self-supporting community.

It's well to be able to remember the villages that were shod by the shoemaker and served by the local butcher and the keeper of the general store, where a farmer sold " fleet " milk to his staff at a halfpenny, or, at most, a penny a quart, and the miller ground the gleanings that the women gathered with so much painstaking. There was no money, hunger was never far away, but the tireless industry of the farm labourer and his wife held the home together. Nothing was wasted ; all the wild fruits of the earth, all Nature's gifts were gathered and though there was little more meat than the poached rabbit could provide, and although in the dim background of their lives stood the grim gaunt workhouse, men and women were of good heart, a stouter generation than their successors can provide.